D0461433

MICROBES

Discover an Unseen World
with 25 PROJECTS

Christine Burillo-Kirch, PhD
Illustrated by Tom Casteel

~ Latest science titles in the *Build It Yourself* Series ~

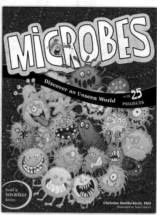

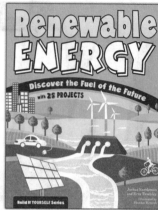

Check out more titles at www.nomadpress.net

Nomad Press
A division of Nomad Communications
10 9 8 7 6 5 4 3 2 1

This book was manufactured by Marquis Book Printing,
Montmagny, Québec, Canada
October 2015, Job #115325
ISBN Softcover: 978-1-61930-310-2
ISBN Hardcover: 978-1-61930-306-5

Illustrations by Tom Casteel
Educational Consultant, Marla Conn

Questions regarding the ordering of this book should be addressed to
Nomad Press
2456 Christian St.
White River Junction, VT 05001
www.nomadpress.net
Printed in Canada.

To Marco and Catherine, my beloved family, with lots of love. To my brother,
Marc, Mom, Dad, Melissa, Jack, and Alex with lots of love. To Nora, Andrea, Den,
Ken, Bren, and Sue for friendship. To Lyn and Deb for the compost bin design.
To Andi and Susan at Nomad Press for their support and guidance.

CONTENTS

INTERESTED IN PRIMARY SOURCES?

Look for this icon. Use a smartphone or tablet app to scan the QR code and explore more about microbes! You can find a list of URLs on the Resources page.

If the QR code doesn't work, try searching the Internet with the Keyword Prompts to find other helpful sources. `microbiology` 🔍

4000–3000 BCE
Egyptians use salt to preserve meat and fish against microbes.

1546
Dr. Girolamo Fracastoro discusses "contagions," which later are known as pathogenic microbes.

1677
Antonie van Leeuwenhoek looks at bodily fluids using a simple hand-held microscope. He names them "animalicules," or "little animals."

1665
Robert Hooke draws pictures of microbes seen with magnifying lenses.

1796
Dr. Edward Jenner develops the first successful vaccine.

1858
French chemist Dr. Louis Pasteur demonstrates the connection between milk spoilage and microbes.

1876
Dr. Robert Koch lays down laws of microbiology that shape much of modern medicine.

1862
Dr. Pasteur successfully convinces scientists that microbes can only arise from parent microbes.

1928
Dr. Alexander Fleming discovers penicillin, the first antibiotic.

1957
Dr. Jonas Salk develops a vaccine using a portion of the polio virus.

1950s–1970s
Many different scientists discover new antibiotics.

1977
Dr. Carl Woese defines a new group of life called "archaea."

1979
Smallpox is the first infection to be declared "eradicated" from the world.

2014
The world's largest outbreak of Ebola occurs in West Africa.

1983
Scientists discover that the HIV virus causes acquired immune deficiency syndrome (AIDS).

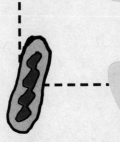

2015
Researchers find that almost half of the DNA found on the surfaces of the New York City subway system do not match any known organism.

INTRODUCTION

MICROBES EVERYWHERE!

Making cheese moldy is a ton of fun.

Sick with a cold?
You can thank me for that!

It takes me a million years to make the oil that fuels your family's car.

I can live in extreme **environments**, such as hot volcanic vents deep in the ocean.

Who am I? A **microbe**!

• • • • • • • WHAT ARE MICROBES? • • • • • • •

Take a look at your arm. Do you see anything on it? Any little creatures eating, moving, or communicating on your skin? Unless you have a microscope, you won't be able to see them, but there are microbes everywhere—on your skin, in the air, in the food you eat, even inside your body! The word *micro* means small, so we know that microbes are small things. Most microbes are so small that we can't see them without microscopes.

WORDS TO KNOW

environment: the area in which something lives.

microbe: a tiny living or nonliving thing.

1

WORDS TO KNOW

organism: any living thing.

microorganism: a living thing that is so small you can only see it with a microscope.

reproduce: to make something new, just like itself.

categorize: to put things into different groups based on their characteristics.

cell: the most basic part of a living thing. Billions of cells make up a plant or animal.

waste: garbage.

The world of microbes includes both living and nonliving things. A living thing is called an **organism**. Living microbes are called **microorganisms**. Microbes are the world's smallest organisms and include bacteria, fungi, protists, and archaea. Viruses are nonliving microbes.

How do we know whether a microbe is living or nonliving? Let's define what makes something alive. When we think of a living thing, we think of something that can eat, breathe, grow, and **reproduce**. Microorganisms can eat, breathe, grow, and reproduce, therefore we can **categorize** them as living.

Microorganisms are made of one or more **cells**. They do not have a mouth to eat with as humans do, but they can pull in food and water across their surfaces. There is no nose to smell with, but microorganisms can follow chemical signals that direct them where to find food. They can also release their **waste** into their environment. Microorganisms cannot talk like we do, but by sending chemical messages, they can communicate with each other.

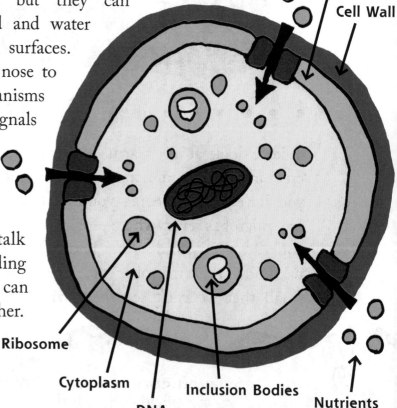

Cell Membrane

Cell Wall

Ribosome

Cytoplasm

DNA

Inclusion Bodies

Nutrients

2

WORDS TO KNOW

ecosystem: a community of living and nonliving things. Living things are plants, animals, and insects. Nonliving things are soil, rocks, and water.

symbiont: a microorganism that exists in harmony with another organism. Both gain benefits from this relationship.

infect: to invade, to cause someone or something to become sick.

pathogen: a microbe that exists only to take advantage of other organisms. Pathogens can cause disease or even death in that organism.

All microbes want to do is make more copies of themselves!

Nonliving microbes, such as viruses, are not dead, but they aren't capable of doing anything on their own. They can't eat or reproduce. You can think of nonliving microbes as sleeping. Viruses wake up when they are in the right environment, which helps them perform different tasks.

Most microbes help their environment. These microbes do good things and even protect us! They help us digest food, provide us with medicines, and keep **ecosystems**, such as lakes and forests, working properly. Without microbes to digest dead plant matter, our forests would be just a big pile of leaves. Microbes that cooperate with and help their environment are called **symbionts**.

Unfortunately, some microbes are destructive. These microbes are a nuisance because they can **infect** us. These harmful microbes are called **pathogens**.

Can you remember a time when you stayed in bed because you felt sick? If you are too sick to get out of bed, you are probably infected with a pathogen. When you feel weak, your body is busy fighting off bad microbes!

3

MICROBES

Even though we can't see them, microbes are everywhere in our daily lives.

Microbe	Living	Visible	Pathogen or Symbiont	Example
Virus	no	no	pathogen	Ebola: causes infection and sometimes death
Bacteria	yes	no	both	*E. coli*: lives in our intestine
Archaea	yes	no	symbiont	*Methanopyrus*: lives in hot hydrothermal vents
Fungi	yes	some types	both	Yeast: used to make bread and pizza dough
Protist	yes	some types	both	Algae: makes oil that we can use to fuel our cars

We need special microscopes to be able to see microbes. Light microscopes can magnify objects thousands of times, while electron microscopes can magnify objects millions of times.

If our eyesight improved one million times, we would be able to see microbes on dust particles, doorknobs, and our skin. Microorganisms are important to the world's ecosystems on land and in water. They might even be able to live in outer space!

4

• • • • • • • A MICRO HISTORY • • • • • • •

If we can't see microbes, how did people discover them? Let's take a quick journey through history. Long before refrigeration, people noticed that their food would stay fresh for only a short period of time before turning rotten. The ancient Egyptians added salt to their fish and meat to prevent it from spoiling, but they didn't understand why this worked.

It took many imaginative and observant individuals to piece together scientific information on microbes.

spoilage: rotting or rotted.

dehydrate: to take the water out of something.

SALT PRESERVATION

How does salt preserve food? In 1858, Dr. Louis Pasteur first made the connection between **spoilage** and microbes. We now know how salt stops most bacteria, mold, and fungus from spoiling food. It weakens or **dehydrates** these microbes so they can't grow on food.

In the 1500s, Dr. Girolamo Fracastoro called microbes "**contagions**," or unseen infecting particles. People still couldn't see microbes, but imagined their presence as the reason illnesses spread between people.

In the 1600s, Robert Hooke and Antonie van Leeuwenhoek developed instruments that allowed them to actually see some microbes. They provided detailed illustrations and descriptions that captivated people's interest in these tiny living things. But there was still no way to control them, and many people died from different illnesses caused by microbes.

In the 1700s, Dr. Edward Jenner made the first successful **vaccine**, for smallpox. This vaccine was used to prevent people from becoming infected.

The smallpox vaccine saved many lives, just as the vaccines we use today save lives.

In the 1800s, Dr. Louis Pasteur showed that microbes were the reason for food spoilage. He also showed that microbes could only come from parent microbes. Before his work, it was thought that microbes magically arose out of thin air!

WORDS TO KNOW

antibiotic: a medicine that can disable or kill bacteria.

theory: an unproven scientific idea.

Did You Know?

When he became president in 1801, Thomas Jefferson was very involved in advocating that Americans get the vaccine for smallpox.

The twentieth century saw many discoveries of medicines that kill or prevent infection from microbes. Dr. Alexander Fleming discovered penicillin, the first **antibiotic**, in 1937. Scientists discovered many more antibiotics in the 1950s through the 1970s.

Today, scientists know a lot about microbes, but there is still plenty to discover! Researchers continue to work at finding cures for illnesses caused by different microbes. The more we understand about microbes, the more we can use them to improve our health and prevent them from making us sick.

Who knows what scientists in our century will discover? Scientific discovery is an ongoing process. Scientists are always making new discoveries based on previous observations from different scientists. No single scientist is responsible for discovering microbes. Scientific discoveries build on each other, and all are important, even the smallest ones. Important scientific discoveries are happening right now—new discoveries are even challenging older scientific **theories**.

DO YOUR OWN MICROBIAL EXPERIMENTS

It's interesting to read about microbes, but it's even more fun to discover microbes yourself! In this book you'll become a microbe hunter and find them in your back yard, nearby pond, and even on your body. These fascinating organisms won't stay hidden once you know how to find and grow them!

GOOD SCIENCE PRACTICES

Every good scientist keeps a science journal! Scientists use the scientific method to keep their experiments organized. Choose a notebook to use as your science journal. As you read through this book and do the activities, keep track of your observations and record each step in a scientific method worksheet, like the one shown here.

Each chapter of this book begins with an essential question to help guide your exploration of microbes.

Question: What are we trying to find out? What problem are we trying to solve?
Research: What do other people think?
Hypothesis/Prediction: What do we think the answer will be?
Equipment: What supplies are we using?
Method: What procedure are we following?
Results: What happened?
Discussion: Why did the results happen?

? ESSENTIAL QUESTION

Keep the question in your mind as you read the chapter. At the end of each chapter, use your science journal to record your thoughts and answers.

TRACK A VIRAL INFECTION MAP

Infection from a virus is called a viral infection. It can be transmitted from person to person. Do you know how many people can be infected from one person? Let's find out!

1 Mr. Donotlike Germs is infected with the Hairy Finger Virus! This virus is infectious for 10 days. Mr. Germs shook Mrs. Leeve Mealone's hand and now, 24 hours later, she is sick! If every infected person infects only one other person per day, and each newly sick person is infectious on the day after they become infected for 10 days, the viral infection path would look like this:

Day 0

Day 1

Day 2

?

Day 3

2 Continue drawing the viral infection path to day 10. How many people are infected on day 7? How many days until 300 people are infected?

THINK MORE: Most people see more than just one person each day. Think about how many people you meet every day, and imagine if all of those people became infected with a virus. What would the numbers look like after five days, ten days, and twenty days in this scenario? What if only half of the people exposed to a virus get infected? How could this happen and how would this change the spread of infection? Why is it so hard to stop viruses from spreading? Is it easier to contain viruses in cities or in the countryside? Why?

CHAPTER 1
THE WORLD OF MICROBES

Let's enter the microscopic world of microbes! Some microbes are so small that thousands, even millions, of them could fit into the period at the end of this sentence. But don't let that fool you. Microbes might be small, but they have important jobs to do and many ecosystems depend on them.

WORDS TO KNOW

DNA: the acronym for deoxyribonucleic nucleic acid. DNA is genetic material that contains instructions that makes us who we are.

classify: to put things in groups based on what they have in common.

Microbes are different from anything else in the natural world, but some microbes are quite similar to certain plants. In fact, until about 40 years ago, some microbes were thought to be part of the plant kingdom. Then scientists realized that microbes have different **DNA** structures from plants, so scientists **classified** microbes in their own groups based on their DNA.

? ESSENTIAL QUESTION

What kinds of environments do different types of microbes live in?

Let's take a closer look at five different types of microbes: viruses, bacteria, fungi, protists, and archaea.

• • • • • • VIRUSES • • • • •

The study of viruses is called **virology**. Viruses are very different from any other microbe. They are all pathogens, which means they are **infectious** and can cause disease. They infect an area and make more copies of themselves. That's their only job! Once they have infected one area, they find a new area and start the process all over again.

Viruses come in a few shapes, such as circles, **polyhedrons**, and rods. The outside shell of every virus contains proteins. Inside each virion, or virus particle, is either DNA or **RNA**. The DNA or RNA of a virus is simply **genetic** material that has instructions for making more of that particular virus.

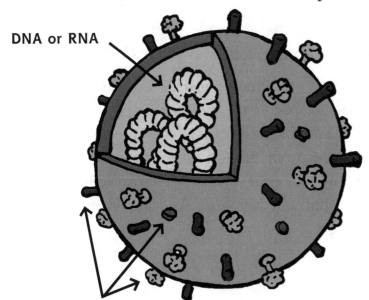

DNA or RNA

Proteins

Do you remember how we decide whether something is living or nonliving? Viruses cannot eat, breathe, or reproduce on their own. Are they living or nonliving?

Viruses get passed from sick people to healthy people in several different ways. Let's follow one path that a virus can take.

What do you do when you sneeze? Ideally, you cover your nose and mouth with your elbow and use a tissue! When you sneeze while you are sick, tiny little droplets of moisture containing the virus are spread into the air. If a sick person sneezes into their hand and then touches a doorknob, there is a good chance that the virus is now on the doorknob. If a healthy person touches the same doorknob and then touches their mouth, nose, eye, or ear, they might become sick from that virus.

Viruses travel from one **host** to another through different bodily **secretions**. These are left behind in the air or on the surfaces of things by a sick person. That's why people need to wash their hands a lot during cold and flu season!

Viruses infect different hosts, including humans, animals, bacteria, and some plants. Animals, plants, and bacteria can all be infected by different viruses, but usually they can't be infected by exactly the same one. One virus will be able to infect cats, but not humans. Another virus can infect humans, but not dogs.

WORDS TO KNOW

host: an organism that can be infected by a microbe.

secretions: fluid produced by our bodies.

Did You Know?

A virus can change to be able to infect two different types of organisms. Scientists believe that a virus first infected monkeys and then changed to human immunodeficiency virus (HIV) to infect humans.

Viruses can exist outside a host for only a short time before **disintegrating**. However, a virus can exist for years inside certain hosts. A host that keeps a virus inside it, but does not get sick, is called a **reservoir**.

Viruses are transmitted from host to host. Upon entering a new host's body, the first thing a virus does is try to find the right cell. A certain type of cell will have just the right environment for the virus to "wake up." Remember, viruses are nonliving microbes. They aren't dead, but they aren't active until they find themselves in the right conditions.

WORDS TO KNOW

disintegrate: the process of falling apart and being destroyed.

reservoir: a host, such as an animal, plant, insect, or person, that maintains, but does not get sick from, a microbe.

epidemic: the rapid spread of a microbe that causes a large population of people to become sick in a short period of time.

RESERVOIR BATS

You might have heard about the Ebola virus in the news. Ebola has infected many people and killed thousands. Scientists believe that bats might be a reservoir for Ebola. This **epidemic** might have been started when a person came in contact with infected bats. In order to combat future epidemics, researchers are currently testing several Ebola vaccines. Maybe there will be a vaccine for Ebola by the time you read this book.

CELLS

Most microbes are single-cell organisms, which means they are made of just one cell. Plants, animals, and humans are made up of millions, even billions of cells! Many different types of cells come together to make an organ, such as the heart. Organs then come together to make systems, such as the circulatory system, which uses blood to carry oxygen and **nutrients** to all parts of our bodies. Different systems come together to help humans, animals, and plants live and function. Watch this short video about cells. What does it make you think about life on Earth?

Bill Nye on cells 🔍

WORDS TO KNOW

nutrients: substances in food and soil that living things need to live and grow.

receptor: a protein on a cell that serves as a lock by interacting with a viral key.

When a virus finds a cell it recognizes as having the right environment, it finds a lock called a **receptor** on the outside of the cell. Sometimes a virus will have the right protein key on its surface. With the right protein key, a virus can unlock the cell and enter it.

All organisms are made of cells.

Once inside the cell, the virus begins its job of forcing the cell to help it make copies of the virus. It makes the host cell follow the instructions encoded in the viral DNA or RNA to make viral parts that assemble into new viruses.

Soon there are so many viral copies made that the virus leaves to find a new host cell to start the process all over again!

14

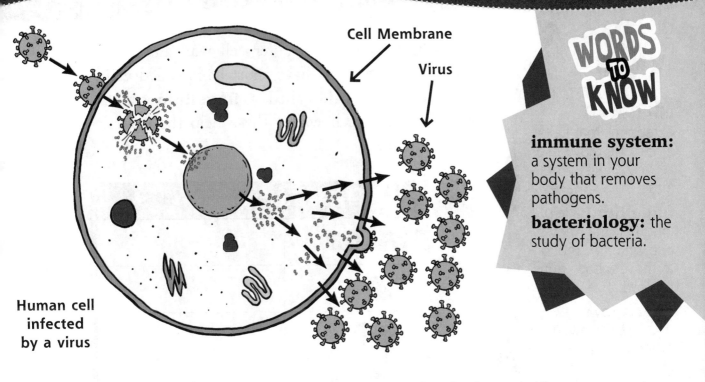

Cell Membrane

Virus

Human cell infected by a virus

Luckily, the host cell has a few ways of defending itself against the virus. While the virus is busy making sure the cell is producing viral copies, the cell steals some of these newly made viral parts and displays them outside, just like you might hang a flag outside your house. With this flag, the infected cell signals to the **immune system**, "Help! I'm infected!" Usually the immune system tries to stop the viral infection by destroying the infected cell and the virus within it. We'll learn how the immune system fights microbes, such as viruses, in Chapter 6.

Did You Know?

You can watch a video showing how a flu virus attacks your body.

flu virus attack NPR 🔍

• • • • • • BACTERIA • • • • • •

The study of bacteria is called **bacteriology**. Bacteria are living microbes. Most can only be seen with the help of an electron microscope or light microscope. Bacteria are generally larger than viruses. They come in many different shapes, such as rods, spheres, and spirals.

WORDS TO KNOW

cilia: hair-like extensions that help a microbe move in a certain direction or attach to a surface.

flagellum: a very long hair that moves in a whip-like motion to move a bacterium forward.

endospore: a small, inactive version of a bacterium that can survive harsh conditions.

All bacteria have an outer cell wall and DNA inside. Some bacteria have short hairs called **cilia** or a very long hair called a **flagellum** on the outside of their cell walls. These help the bacteria move around.

Bacteria Cell Shapes	
▬	rod
●	sphere
●●	double sphere
～～	spiral

Certain bacteria can make living **endospores** if they encounter a harsh environment or if a food source disappears. An endospore is a version of the bacterium that contains all its genetic information in a compact structure that can withstand heat, cold, harsh chemicals, dryness, and radiation. The endospore doesn't eat or grow. It's asleep, waiting to be revived.

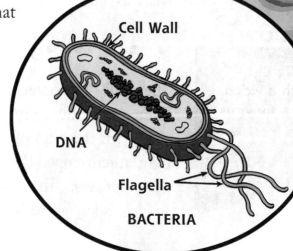

Cell Wall

DNA

Flagella

BACTERIA

16

YOU'RE HOW OLD?!

In 1995, a group of scientists in the Dominican Republic extracted and revived a bacterial endospore from a bee encased in amber that was 25 to 30 million years old. In 2000, another study revived a 250-million-year-old bacterial endospore from salt crystals found in Carlsbad, New Mexico. Both studies checked the DNA to find out the approximate ages of both samples. Does this mean that bacterial endospores can live forever? What do you think?

When the endospore reaches a better environment, it can turn back into an active bacterium that can grow, eat, and reproduce.

WORDS TO KNOW

aerobic: an environment with oxygen.

anaerobic: an environment with low oxygen or no oxygen.

Bacteria live in many different places. They exist in water, soil, animals, insects, our intestines, on our skin, and on plants.

Bacteria do not like to live where it is too hot, too cold, or too salty. Many bacteria can live in an **aerobic** environment that has oxygen, and others can live in an **anaerobic** environment that has little or no oxygen. Bacteria usually travel by being passed from host to host, similar to how viruses are transferred. Some can move short distances with the help of a flagellum or cilia.

Did You Know?

Although you usually hear about bacteria making us sick, most bacteria are either symbiotic or hardly interact with us at all. Very few bacteria are pathogenic!

WORDS TO KNOW

decomposer: any organism that breaks down dead or decaying organic matter.

organic: something that is or was living.

susceptible: easily influenced or affected by something.

Bacteria can be symbionts, pathogens, or **decomposers** in different ecosystems. Like viruses, some bacteria can survive in a reservoir host without hurting or helping the host.

Bacteria that are symbiotic help their host survive. Symbiotic bacteria, such as some of the lactic acid bacteria found in yogurt, have a mutually beneficial relationship with humans. The bacteria makes humans healthier after eating the yogurt, and the bacteria gains a comfortable place to live—inside a human body!

Pathogenic bacteria can infect plants, animals, microbes, and humans. Salmonella is a pathogen that can make humans and animals sick. This is a bacteria that can be found in some raw eggs and other food.

Bacteria called decomposers work with fungi to digest leaves or other dead **organic** material. The word *decompose* means to rot and decay, which is considered a bad thing when we're talking about the apples in your fruit bowl, but in this case it's a good thing! Decomposers return nutrients to the soil to support the growth of plants and trees.

Good bacteria live in all of our bodily secretions, such as the mucus in our noses and mouths. When we're sick, harmful bacteria join the good bacteria in these secretions.

Did You Know?

To treat a bacterial infection, such as pneumonia, a doctor might prescribe an antibiotic. Antibiotics can help if the pathogenic bacteria are **susceptible** to the antibiotic. Susceptible bacteria have certain properties that an antibiotic can use to help destroy them.

18

HOW ENLIGHTENING!

The bacterium *Vibrio fischeri* has a symbiotic relationship with squid that is very enlightening! It **colonizes** its squid host's light organ when the squid is newly hatched. The bacteria are **luminescent** and give the squid the ability to produce light. In this symbiotic relationship, the squid can glow in the dark and scare off **predators**, while the bacteria have a safe home!

• • • • • • FUNGI • • • • • • •

Fungi are a large, diverse group of living microbes that includes mushrooms, mold, lichens, and yeast. Scientists estimate that there might be a million different **species** of fungi, but only about 100,000 of them have been characterized so far. The study of fungi is called **mycology**.

Many fungi are useful and some are quite tasty! Do you like to eat mushrooms in your omelets? You're eating fungi! The yeast that makes bread or pizza dough rise is also part of the fungi family. Remember to thank the fungi family next time you gobble down a slice of mushroom pizza. Several medicines come from fungi as well.

WORDS TO KNOW

colonize: to move into and live in.

luminescent: glowing.

predator: an animal that hunts another animal for food.

species: a group of plants or animals that are closely related and look the same.

mycology: the study of fungi.

19

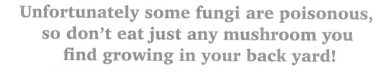

parasitic: living on another plant or animal and feeding off of it.

hyphae: long shapes on some fungi that serve as the main place of growth.

mycelium: a large web of hyphae.

Unfortunately some fungi are poisonous, so don't eat just any mushroom you find growing in your back yard!

Fungi are everywhere. They live in soil, ponds, the air, food, and symbiotically in human bodies. Although plants get the minerals they need through symbiotic relationships with fungi, some fungi are **parasitic** to plants. A person might become infected with parasitic fungi if their immune system is not working properly.

Did You Know?

Fungi were once classified as part of the Plant Kingdom, but are now considered a separate group despite sharing some similar features with plants.

You probably know what a mushroom looks like, but have you ever looked closely at fungi growing at the base of a tree? Most fungi, such as mold and lichen, grow long rod shapes called **hyphae** that cannot be seen without a microscope. The hyphae consist of lots of similar cells lined up next to each other to form a rod-like extension. A large network or mesh of hyphae form a **mycelium**. Have you ever seen fuzzy bread mold? That's a mycelium!

Lichens and yeast look different from other members of the Fungi Kingdom. Lichens have a more complex structure because of their symbiotic relationship with algae. Lichens have layers of hyphae, plus layers of algae or cyanobacteria, or both. Yeast grow as single cells.

Fungi feed mostly on other organisms, but some can make their own food. Fungi digest their food outside of their body. They excrete **enzymes** on whatever they are trying to eat. These enzymes break up the food into digestible particles that fungi will then consume. Can you imagine spitting on a piece of food and waiting for it to turn soggy before eating it? That's what fungi do!

Like plants, most fungi are **immobile**. However, some are able to make and release **spores** called **conidia**. Stored in a structure called a fruiting body, spores are colorful, dust-like particles that are lifted into the air and carried to new destinations. They contain all the genetic information needed to make a new fungus.

WORDS TO KNOW

enzyme: a protein that speeds up a chemical reaction.

immobile: not capable of moving.

spore: a single cell that can produce an organism.

conidia: colorful spores released by fungi that enable the fungi to grow in a different area.

Most fungi are decomposers. Fungi will digest any organic material, such as dead leaves, trees, animals, and insects.

This is an extremely important job that fungi share with certain bacteria. Decomposition returns nutrients from leaves and dead organic matter back to the soil. Can you imagine the enormous amount of leaves that would pile up in our forests without decomposers to break them down?

•PROTISTS•

The study of protists is called **protistology**. Protists live mostly in water, but they can also be found in insect and animal intestines. Members of the protist group include red, brown, and green algae, diatoms, plankton, protozoa, paramecium, and slime molds, as well as many other organisms.

Protists can be single-celled or multicellular. All protists have DNA inside their cells. Large protists, such as seaweeds, are multicellular. Seaweeds have thousands of the same type of cell networked together into a sheet, or **filamented** structure.

A small protist, such as a paramecium, is composed of a single cell. Many protists are immobile, but some single-cell protists have cilia, flagella, or pseudopods that they can use to push themselves forward.

Did You Know?

Pseudopod means *fake foot*. Some protists have pseudopods that they use to temporarily grab onto a surface and propel themselves forward!

PS VOMIT OR SLIME MOLD?

It may be hard to believe, but there is a slime mold that scientists affectionately call "dog vomit slime mold." *Fuligo septica* is a yellowish slime mold that can grow on mulch in the garden, especially after long periods of rain. If you do find it in your back yard, handle it with care. It is not poisonous, but its spores can set off allergies or asthma if you are allergic to it. Take a look at a picture of *Fuligo septica*. Do you think it looks like vomit?

dog vomit slime mold 🔍

vector: something that can carry a microbe from one organism to another.

photosynthesis: the process of using light and carbon dioxide to make food and energy for the organism.

Pseudopod

Unfortunately, several protists cause sickness in humans. Malaria, amoebic dysentery, and African sleeping sickness are a few of the diseases that are caused by parasitic protists. If parasitic protists live in the water and in insect intestines, how do they infect us?

Parasitic protists infect humans by using a **vector**. For example, in areas of the world that have temperatures above 68 degrees Fahrenheit (20 degrees Celsius) year round, the protist *Plasmodium* uses mosquitos as vectors to infect humans and cause malaria. When a mosquito lands on someone's skin, it injects some of its saliva into the blood vessel before starting to suck out its meal. If that mosquito is carrying plasmodium, that protist gets put into the unknowing person, who will then become infected and get sick with malaria.

Most protists make their own food by photosynthesis, just as plants do. **Photosynthesis** changes sunlight into chemical energy, making sugars that the organism can use for fuel. Some protists, though, cannot make their own food and need to eat other organisms. One particular protist, a paramecium, will eat harmful bacteria.

If you've ever eaten a sushi roll with nori, or seaweed, you have eaten a protist!

23

ARCHAEA

Some microbes love extreme **habitats**, such as very hot or salty environments, and they even need to live in these habitats. Scientists used to think that these were just odd bacteria.

WORDS TO KNOW

habitat: a plant or animal's home, which supplies it with food, water, and shelter.

thermophile: a heat-loving organism.

halophile: a salt-loving organism.

methanogen: an organism that produces methane gas.

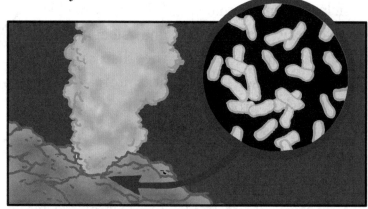

Archaea living near a hydrothermal vent

In the 1970s, researchers discovered that these microbes had different sequences in certain molecules when compared to bacteria. So they were placed in their own group called *archaea*, which means *primitive*. There are three kinds of archaea.

- **Thermophiles** can tolerate heat up to 194 degrees Fahrenheit (90 degrees Celsius).

- **Halophiles** can live in water that contains 30 percent salt!

- **Methanogens** like to live in anaerobic environments where they produce stinky methane gas.

Many microbes can't survive high heat or salt. Remember how food is preserved? Bacteria shrivel up in salt and can be destroyed in high heat. Archaea, however, have unique cell walls and enzymes that allow them to live in very harsh environments. Their cell walls have a chemical composition not seen anywhere else in the world, which is strong enough to stand up to harsh climates.

24

The enzymes of archaea have strong chemical bonds that allow them to function in hot temperatures.

Have you watched an egg fry in a pan? The egg white changes from clear to white due to the proteins in the egg white unraveling from the heat. A normal enzyme disintegrates and loses the ability to function under high heat. Not so for an archaean enzyme!

HOT, SALTY, AND STINKY

How would you like to live at the surface of a hot vent in the deep ocean? How about in Yellowstone Park inside a hot sulfur spring? If you were a member of the archaean group, these are places that you would call home! Thermophiles live in hot volcanic vents. Halophiles love to live in the Great Salt Lake in the United States, where the water can contain as much as 30 percent salt.

Methanogens live in anaerobic environments found in both freshwater and ocean habitats. Methanogens also live in cow, rabbit, horse, and termite intestines, and sometimes in human intestines, where they produce a lot of methane gas. Guess where that gas goes? Out into the environment. Unfortunately, methane gas is a **greenhouse gas** that contributes to **global warming**.

WORDS TO KNOW

greenhouse gas: a gas such as water vapor, **carbon dioxide**, or methane that traps heat and contributes to warming temperatures.

carbon dioxide: an odorless, colorless gas formed from the burning of fossil fuels, the rotting of dead plants and animals, and when animals breathe out.

global warming: an increase in the average temperature of the earth's atmosphere, enough to cause climate change.

Archaea are similar in size to bacteria. Scientists need electron microscopes to see them. Some archaea have a rod, sphere, or spiral shape. A few archaea look very different from any other microbe.

Some halophiles actually have a square shape!

Some archaea have flagella to move around, while some cannot move at all. All archaea have DNA inside them that contains their genetic instructions.

Archaea coexist in many environments in a symbiotic manner. Methanogens have been found in the human gut, and they have not been known to cause sickness in people. Halophiles are found on high-salt foods such as sausages and fish, but generally are harmless. Most of us will probably never encounter a thermophile!

Now that you know a little bit about each type of microbe, let's start looking for them.

CONSIDER THE ESSENTIAL QUESTION

Write your thoughts about this chapter's Essential Question in your science journal, using information you've gathered from reading and knowledge you may already have. Share it with other students and friends. Did you all come up with the same answers? What is different? Do this for every chapter.

? **ESSENTIAL QUESTION**

What kinds of environments do different types of microbes live in?

ARCHAEAN SUPERHERO

IDEAS FOR SUPPLIES
drawing materials

Archaea love extreme environments, including places that are very salty, boiling hot, or without oxygen. In some ways, they're like superheroes who can withstand extremes, such as one who can breathe underwater or one who likes it very cold. Create your own superhero microbe based on archaea!

1 Brainstorm the characteristics of your superhero microbe. Here are some questions to get you started.

* What extreme environment does your superhero live in?

* What does your superhero microbe look like?

* What super powers are you going to give it?

* How about a costume or special gear to survive?

2 Use the sample step-by-step guide below to help you draw your superhero performing incredible feats of bravery. Don't forget to test it out in its extreme environment!

BACTERIAL INCUBATOR

IDEAS FOR SUPPLIES
cardboard box (at least 12 inches by 12 inches)
✳ *aluminum foil* ✳ *aluminum tape (sold in hardware stores)*

Before we can do experiments with bacteria, we need to build a cozy place for them to grow. In a scientific lab, bacterial **cultures** grow in an instrument called an incubator. This is a large metal container with a door that supplies the best temperature, **atmosphere**, and **humidity** for bacteria to grow on **media plates**. Your incubator will maintain heat. Atmosphere and humidity are more difficult to control, and we will not worry about them here.

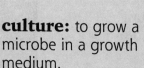

WORDS TO KNOW

culture: to grow a microbe in a growth medium.

atmosphere: the blanket of air surrounding the earth.

humidity: the amount of moisture in the air.

media plate: a dish that contains a growth medium for growing microbes in a laboratory.

1 Seal the bottom flaps of your box with tape so that it remains closed. Cut off the two short top flaps and one long top flap. Make sure to leave one long flap attached to the box.

2 To make a door, tape the long flap that you cut off to the long flap that is still attached to the box so it reaches all the way across the box.

3 Turn the box and place it with the door facing forward. Cover each part of the inside of the box with aluminum foil. Use aluminum tape to secure the foil to all the edges and corners. Don't forget to cover the inside of the door, too!

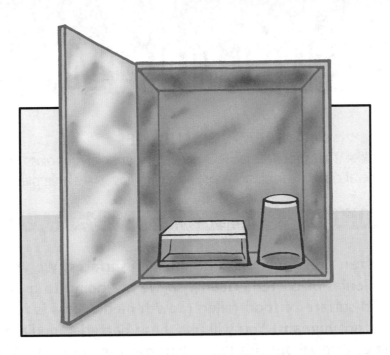

⚡ Make a sign and attach it to the front so people know that your incubator is scientific equipment and not recycling!

THINK MORE: Why do you want the entire inside of the box covered in foil?

STERILITY

Sterility is a level of cleanliness in which an object or area is free of microbes. The process of sterilization kills all microbes on an object or in an area. An object is sterilized by either using very high heat, liquid or gas forms of certain chemicals, high pressure, or high-level **filtration**. Do you think that there are areas in our home that are **sterile**? Why or why not?

WORDS TO KNOW

filtration: passing liquid through a filter to clean it of particles.

sterile: free from microorganisms.

29

BACTERIAL MEDIA PLATES

IDEAS FOR SUPPLIES

chicken stock ✳ 1 teaspoon sugar ✳ 3 packets plain gelatin ✳ glass measuring cup ✳ several clean clear plastic containers with lids ✳ sealable plastic bags

SAFETY TIP: Have an adult help you with hot liquids.

Bacteria can grow in liquids and on solid surfaces. We want to see the colonies of bacteria clearly, so we are going to grow them on a solid surface of food called growth media. This is food for bacteria, not humans! You will use these bacterial media plates in activities throughout this book. You can use your media plates to find microbes in your house! Make sure that you throw away media plates when you are done using them in each experiment.

Once we have created the media plates, it is very important to store them in an inverted, or upside down, position. Moisture often accumulates on the inside of containers. If we store the plates in an upright position, the bacterial colonies will be unrecognizable because they will be a big gooey mess!

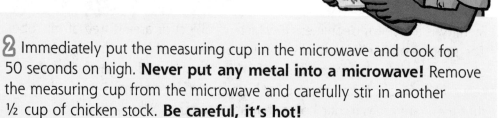

1 Combine ½ cup of chicken stock, sugar, and all gelatin in the glass measuring cup. Mix with a spoon.

2 Immediately put the measuring cup in the microwave and cook for 50 seconds on high. **Never put any metal into a microwave!** Remove the measuring cup from the microwave and carefully stir in another ½ cup of chicken stock. **Be careful, it's hot!**

3 Pour about half an inch of the mixture into each plastic container. Put the lids on top without sealing them. If you press the lid down tight, the heat will cause the pressure to build up and the top will pop off. Place the containers in an area where they can sit undisturbed for one hour.

4 After one hour, firmly seal the containers. Put your media containers in the refrigerator upside down in a sealable bag. You can use the refrigerated containers for about two weeks to grow bacterial colonies.

MAKING MEDIA PLATES

Here are a few of suggestions for making your microbe media plates to keep them uncontaminated and ready to use in experiments!

✳ Wash your hands.

✳ Clean the area of the kitchen where you will prepare the media plates.

✳ Pour the microwaved gelatin mixture quickly and neatly.

✳ Place the containers in an area of the kitchen that will remain undisturbed while cooling.

HUNT FOR MICROBES

IDEAS FOR SUPPLIES

plastic wrap ✳ *rubber bands* ✳ *ThermaCare heat wrap (optional)*

**Now that you've made a bacterial incubator
and media plates, you are ready to start hunting
for microbes in your own house.**

1 Take one prepared media plate, remove the lid, and wrap the top with plastic wrap. Use a rubber band to keep the plastic wrap in place. Label the bottom of the container *negative control* and place it in the incubator upside down.

2 Take two other media plates and put them in two different areas of your house with the covers off. These are your experimental plates. Leave them uncovered for six hours.

3 After the six-hour period, cover each container with plastic wrap and a rubber band. Label each container with masking tape indicating the area it was in. Put both containers in the incubator upside down as well. If you have a heat wrap, now is a good time to put it in the incubator. A ThermaCare heat wrap is activated when you take it out of the package.

32

4 In your science journal, write down your experiment title, materials used, and your method. What is your hypothesis? What do you expect your results to look like? What kind of microbes do you think will grow?

5 Look at your plates, but don't unwrap them. Record your results at 24, 48, and 72 hours. Write down how many different types of microbes you see, and the details about the microbes. Are they smooth? Wrinkled? What color are they? You can also draw the results of your experiment.

THINK MORE: Why is it a good idea to store the media plates in the refrigerator until you need them for an experiment? What do you think the bacteria will eat from this media? What other microbe, besides bacteria, might grow on these media plates?

NEGATIVE AND POSITIVE EXPERIMENTAL CONTROLS

A negative control is the part of an experiment that helps you make sure that the materials you are using are free from microbes. It also lets you know that you are performing the experiment correctly. You should not have any microbes growing in your negative control at any time. If you do, then it is best to remake the media containers or think about how you did the experiment. Were your hands dirty while doing the experiment? Did you leave the media containers open for a long period of time? Did any food or hair get in the container?

A positive control is another way to show that the experiment was performed correctly. The positive control uses a known source of bacteria to show that bacterial growth can occur in your experiment. If you don't see growth on a positive control plate, something is wrong with the growth plates. Did you forget a certain ingredient?

FUNGAL BALLOON RACES

IDEAS FOR SUPPLIES

*3 packages yeast * 3 empty bottles * 3 small uninflated balloons * sugar * cold apple juice*

Yeast is a fungus that's used in baking to make bread and cakes nice and light. You can watch yeast in action and discover in what conditions it grows best.

1 Wash your hands first! Pour the contents of one package of yeast (2¼ teaspoons) into each of the three bottles.

2 To make a negative control first, place 1 cup of cold water into a glass measuring cup and microwave for one minute on high. This will make the temperature of the water right for the yeast to grow. Pour the entire cup of water into one bottle with yeast. Quickly take one balloon and firmly place it over the mouth of the bottle. Secure the balloon in place with tape or a rubber band. Label the water bottle *negative control*.

3 To make the positive control, place 1 cup of cold water and 1 tablespoon of sugar into a glass measuring cup and heat in the microwave for one minute on high. Mix the sugar and water with a clean spoon to dissolve all the sugar. Add the solution to the second bottle with yeast. Quickly place a balloon over the mouth of the bottle, secure it in place, and label the bottle *positive control*.

Did You Know ?

Fungi can grow in some amazing ways. Watch this video about the different forms fungi can take.

fungi structure 🔍

4 To create the experimental condition, place 1 cup of cold apple juice into a clean glass measuring cup and heat in the microwave for one minute on high. Pour the warm apple juice into the third bottle with yeast. Quickly place a balloon over the mouth and secure it in place. The bottle should feel slightly warm. Label this bottle *apple juice*.

5 Write up your hypothesis and methods while the experiment is going. This experiment will not take long to finish. What do you notice happening to the balloons? What do you think is going on? What is the sugar doing in the positive control?

THINK MORE: What conditions make the yeast react? Where else can yeast grow? Come up with your own liquid concoction and see if yeast will grow in it!

CREEPY FUNGI

While the bleeding tooth *Hydnellum peckii* fungus is not thought to be poisonous, it certainly might win a prize for "most creepy" looking! This fungus is potentially a source of medicine for people with blood disorders. Take a look at some photos of the bleeding tooth.

Hydnellum peckii 🔍

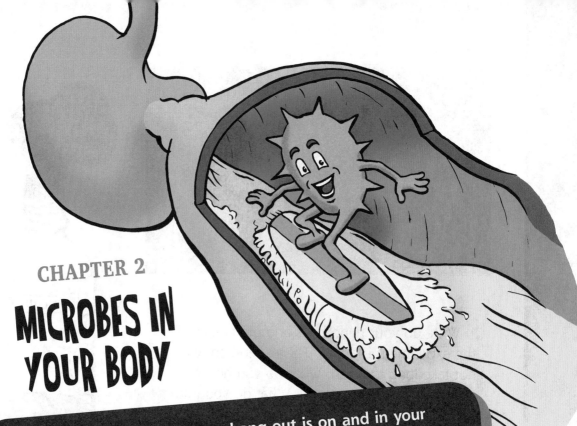

CHAPTER 2

MICROBES IN YOUR BODY

One place microbes love to hang out is on and in your body! Microbes prefer to live in moist places, but they can live in dry areas as well. Your skin has dry areas, such as the palm of your hand, and moist places, such as inside your nostrils. Bacteria, yeast, and fungi live in both these areas on your body. They live in lots of other places in your body, too. You probably have at least 1,000 different kinds of bacteria, five types of yeast, and a fungus living on you right now.

• • • • • • • • GET THE SKINNY • • • • • • •

Now that you know how many kinds of microbes are living on you right now, do you have the urge to run to the shower and try scrubbing them off? Actually, it's healthy and good for you to have that many microbes living on you!

? ESSENTIAL QUESTION

What are microbes doing in and on your body?

36

It might seem as though these microbes are living off of us and giving nothing in return, but they are actually protecting us. These microbes are part of your body's normal **flora**.

One of their jobs is to prevent other harmful bacteria from living on your skin. If a harmful bacterium lands on your skin, your normal flora crowd the pathogen out and prevent it from getting any nutrients.

WORDS TO KNOW

flora: the symbiotic microbes that reside in different parts of the body.

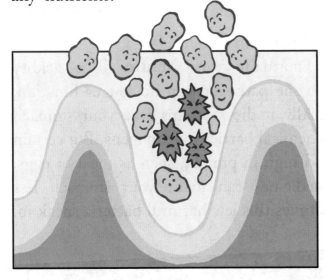

If it weren't for your normal flora, it would be much easier for pathogens to infect you.

Our skin also protects us from harmful pathogens. It serves as a physical barrier and does not allow pathogens to break in unless you have a cut. This is why it is important to treat every cut in your skin with soap, warm water, and a Band-Aid. Always let an adult or someone who has been trained in first aid treat your cut, as they can determine if additional topical medicines are needed.

We also have microbes in our mouth, stomach, and intestines. Let's see what it would be like to be a pathogen on a piece of food. The journey begins in your mouth, where the pathogen encounters normal flora of the mouth and saliva.

37

Saliva not only breaks down your food, it also breaks down bacterial cell walls. Inside the mouth is definitely not a cozy place for a pathogen. If the pathogen survives the attack of saliva, it will journey down to the stomach. Do you think the stomach would be a warm and inviting place for a pathogen?

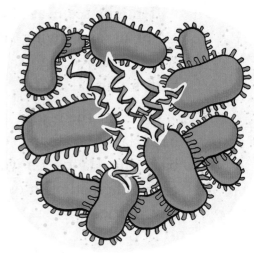

WORDS TO KNOW

acidic: from acids, which are chemical compounds that taste sour, bitter, or tart. Examples are vinegar and lemon juice.

biofilm: a sheet of bacteria.

The condition in your stomach is normally very **acidic**. This acidity makes it so the pathogen can no longer function, and eventually it dies. In this way your stomach provides a chemical barrier to pathogens. But certain types of food high in protein, such as meat or eggs, or certain medicines can make your stomach less acidic. Sometimes this lets harmful bacteria sneak in.

HUMAN OR MICROBE?

Scientists have discovered that we have more microbes on and in our bodies than we have human cells! These microbes have many important jobs to do, including keeping us healthy and able to eat certain types of foods. Some of the microbes are out to do us harm, though, such as the bacteria sticking to your teeth. These develop into a **biofilm** and cause cavities. Don't forget to brush and floss every day! You can see pictures of some of the microbes in our bodies.

human microbes photo

Bacteria can also find ways to defend themselves from stomach acid. To keep us from getting sick from the microbes that live on

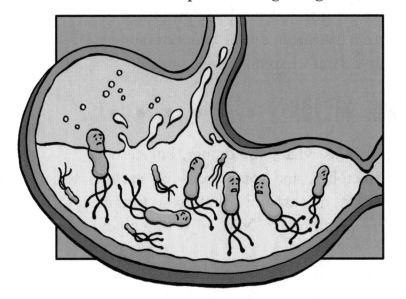

some foods, such as raw meat, we cook our steak, chicken, and fish before eating it. High heat kills off harmful microbes.

If the pathogen survives saliva and the acidity of the stomach, it will next reach the intestines. Friendly bacteria in our intestines protect us.

Scientists estimate that there are more than a trillion bacteria living in our intestines!

These bacteria crowd harmful microbes away from the food sources in our intestines. This is similar to the way bacteria act on our skin.

Intestinal bacteria help us digest cellulose, which is found in lettuce and other vegetables. We wouldn't be able to eat certain foods without them! The normal flora also produces certain vitamins that we need but can't make, such as vitamin K and vitamin B12.

Can you imagine having to survive saliva in a mouth, acid in a stomach, and competition from the microbes that live in our intestines? It's surprising that we get infected at all! Helpful microbes are constantly protecting us from pathogens. Our immune system, which you will learn about in a later chapter, helps too.

• • • • • • • MMMM, MICROBES • • • • • • •

You might not think of microbes as what's for dinner, but certain foods we eat are made with microbes, and some foods we eat are microbes! Have you eaten a mushroom? That is a fungus! Remember that sushi roll with nori? Nori is seaweed and seaweed is a protist!

WORDS TO KNOW

ferment: when microorganisms convert sugars into acids.

Cheese, pickles, sauerkraut, and even chocolate cannot be made without help from bacteria.

Do you like to eat chocolate? Did you know that cocoa beans taste nothing like chocolate? The chocolate taste, as we know it, comes from **fermenting** cocoa beans for almost a week. In fact, unfermented cocoa beans are highly bitter! Let's follow the fermentation process of a cocoa bean.

Cocoa beans are fermented directly on the farm. First, they are removed from the harvested cocoa pod. The beans are placed in a wooden crate between layers of banana leaves, where yeast and lactic acid bacteria attack the pulp surrounding the cocoa beans.

Did You Know?

Sauerkraut is fermented cabbage and pickles are fermented cucumbers!

The yeast and lactic acid bacteria leave behind food products for the next microbial player, the acetic acid bacteria. This bacteria works on part of the seed itself and makes even more fermentation products. After the cocoa beans have gone through the entire fermentation cycle, they are put into the sun to dry. Before long, they will be made into yummy chocolate at a chocolate factory!

WORDS TO KNOW

curdle: when milk protein clumps together due to acidity.

curd: a solid chunk of milk protein.

Cheese is an example of a highly regulated fermented product. Cheese is made by adding lactic acid bacteria to milk. These bacteria ferment the milk sugars until the whole mixture is acidic. The milk protein **curdles** as the mixture turns acidic. These solid milk **curds** can be collected and combined to make cheese. The cheese is then allowed to ferment until the right flavor is achieved.

Lactic acid bacteria can be added to dairy products to make sour cream or to veggies such as cabbage to make sauerkraut! Pickles are fermented cucumbers, using, you guessed it, lactic acid bacteria. Yogurt is made through fermentation of dairy products using a different kind of lactic acid bacteria.

ESSENTIAL QUESTION

Now it's time to consider and discuss the Essential Question:
What are microbes doing in and on your body?

41

COMPARE YOUR HANDPRINTS

IDEAS FOR SUPPLIES
prepared media plates ✳ *plastic wrap* ✳ *heat wrap*

Our hands touch a lot of different things every day, so they are constantly picking up microbes. That's why it's important not to touch your face without washing your hands. For this experiment, don't wash your hands before you start. We'll see what the microbes on your hands look like.

1 Take three media plates out of the refrigerator. Bacteria do not like their growth media to be chilly, so let them sit for an hour at room temperature before starting.

2 While your media plates are warming up, get your hands dirty! Play with your pets, run around outside, and touch lots of different things. The dirtier your hands, the better!

3 Choose a container of bacterial media. Gently place your hand or fingertips on the surface of the media and press firmly. Do not push into the media too hard or some gelatin will break off. Cover the container with plastic wrap and a rubber band. Label the container with your name and the words *dirty hand*. Put this in the incubator upside down. If you have a heat wrap, put it in the incubator.

4 Now wash your hands with soap and water for 20 seconds. Choose a new media plate. Gently place your hand or fingertips on the surface, just as you did with your dirty hand. Cover the container, label it with your name and *clean hand*, and put it in the incubator upside down.

5 To prepare the negative control, label a media plate *negative control*. Remove the lid and wrap the top with plastic wrap and place the negative control in the incubator upside down.

6 Start a scientific method worksheet in your science journal. What is your hypothesis? What kind of microbes do you think will grow and on which plates will they grow?

7 Look at your plates, but don't unwrap them. Record your results at 24, 48, and 72 hours. Record your observations about how many colonies grew and what you notice about each one.

MICROBIAL TRANSPLANTS?

No doubt you've heard about heart and lung transplants, but how about microbial transplants? When a woman was extremely sick from having only pathogenic bacteria in her intestines, she was slowly dying. Many treatments had been tried, such as antibiotics and putting beneficial bacterial stocks in her intestine, but all had failed.

A doctor at the hospital where she was being treated thought, why not perform a microbial transplant? The transplant involved taking microbial flora from her husband's intestine and putting them into her intestine. It worked so well that she was able to leave the hospital 24 hours later!

MOUTH SWABS

4 prepared media plates ✳ *cotton swabs* ✳ *plastic wrap*

What do the bacteria in your mouth look like? Will they be the same or different from the bacteria you found on your hands?

1 Take the prepared media plates out of the refrigerator and let them warm up for one hour at room temperature.

2 Wash your hands! Your experiments won't be sterile, but keeping your hands clean will allow you to get good results.

3 To prepare the negative control, label a media plate *negative control*. Remove the lid and wrap the top with plastic wrap using a rubber band to keep the plastic wrap in place. Place the negative control in the incubator upside down.

4 Take a cotton swab and put it in your mouth against your teeth and gums. Brush the cotton swab back and forth for a good 30 seconds at the gumline.

44

5 Choose a new media plate. Gently place the swab on the surface of the media and swipe it back and forth over the entire surface. Do not push the swab into the media too hard or some gelatin will break off. Throw the swab away into the garbage. Cover the container with plastic wrap and a rubber band. Label this container with your name and *gumline*. Put this in the incubator upside down as well. If you have a heat wrap, now is a good time to put it in the incubator.

6 Take a new swab and simply put the swab in your mouth for a few seconds instead of at the gumline. Prepare a new container and label this one *saliva*.

7 Now go brush and floss your teeth and rinse with mouthwash. Repeat step 4 with a new swab. Put it in your mouth against your teeth and gums. Make sure to brush the cotton swab back and forth for a good 30 seconds at the gumline. Prepare a new media plate and label this one *brushed teeth*.

8 In your science journal, record the details of your experiment and materials in a scientific method worksheet. What is your hypothesis? What kind of microbes do you think will grow and on which plates will they grow?

9 Look at your plates, but don't unwrap them. Record your results at 24, 48, and 72. Record your observations about what grew and what you notice about each one.

THINK MORE: Why do you think you had to brush your cotton swab really well against your gumline? Did brushing and flossing your teeth result in fewer colonies growing or did it not matter? What predictions can you make about how many cavities will develop if you don't brush and floss your teeth?

CULTURE BACTERIA FROM YOGURT

IDEAS FOR SUPPLIES

sugar ✳ 3 packets gelatin ✳ glass measuring cup ✳ milk ✳ 5 clean containers with lids ✳ yogurt ✳ cotton swabs ✳ plastic wrap ✳ large glass jar with metal lid, big enough to hold the 5 containers stacked ✳ tealight candle ✳ matches

Safety tip: Have an adult help you with hot liquids and matches.

WORDS TO KNOW

opaque: not transparent.

Yogurt is made through fermentation of dairy products with a certain kind of lactic acid bacteria. We are going to grow these bacteria from yogurt on special milk growth plates. Normally, these bacteria need very warm temperatures to grow. We have a limited temperature range because we are using gelatin for milk media plates, so these colonies will be small and a bit difficult to see. You will be able to notice that they are there because the milk will curdle and become **opaque** wherever there are bacteria growing!

1 Combine ½ cup of water, 1 teaspoon of sugar, and all the gelatin in a glass measuring cup. Combine quickly by mixing with a spoon. Put the measuring cup in the microwave for 50 seconds on high. **Never put any metal into a microwave!** Remove from the microwave and stir carefully with a clean spoon—**careful, it's hot!**

2 Heat ½ cup of milk in a glass container in the microwave for 30 seconds on high. Immediately pour the warm milk into the gelatin-sugar mixture. Mix well with a spoon.

3 Pour about a half inch of the mixture into each plastic container and place the lids on top without pressing down. If you seal the lid, the heat causes pressure to build up and the top will pop off. Place the containers in an area where they can sit undisturbed for at least two hours.

4 After two hours, shake the water off the lids and firmly seal the tops on each container. Store your milk growth plates in the refrigerator for up to one week. Keep them sterile by sealing them upside down in a plastic bag.

5 Label one milk growth plate *negative control*. Remove the lid and wrap the top with plastic wrap. You can now place one negative control upside down in your glass jar. This will be your anaerobic chamber.

6 Take a swab, open a fresh container of yogurt, and put your swab in the yogurt. Gently place the swab on the surface of a milk media and swipe it back and forth over the entire surface. Cover the container with plastic wrap and label it *yogurt*. Put this into your anaerobic chamber. Do the same for your other milk media plates.

7 Ask an adult to help you prepare the anaerobic chamber. Once all the containers are placed upside down in the chamber, put a tealight candle on top of the containers. Have the adult light a candle and seal the chamber well with the lid. The candle will go out after a minute.

8 Start a scientific method worksheet and record your experiment in your science journal. What do you think will happen to the yogurt culture?

THINK MORE: Why are we growing the bacteria in an anaerobic chamber? Why are we lighting a candle in the chamber? What does it mean when the candle goes out? How else can we make an anaerobic chamber?

GROW MOLD ON LEMONS

IDEAS FOR SUPPLIES
2 lemons ✳ *sealable plastic bags*

This experiment will take several weeks to complete, but it will be worth the wait.

1 With a fork, poke holes in two plastic bags. Label one bag with the date and *refrigerator*. Label the other bag with the date and *cupboard*.

2 Put a lemon in each bag and seal the bags. Put the bag labeled *refrigerator* in your refrigerator. Put the bag labeled *cupboard* in a closed cupboard so it doesn't receive much light.

3 Start a scientific method worksheet and wait for the mold to grow. It may take several weeks! Which lemon will grow mold first? Do not open up the plastic bags—just look at the mold through the closed bags. Save one lemon with mold for a future experiment in Chapter 6. But be sure to double bag it (place the original bag with the lemon into a new bag without holes).

THINK MORE: Grow mold on bread. Do the exact same experiment with fresh bread, under the same conditions. Make sure to sprinkle a tiny bit of water on the bread. Under which condition does mold grow the quickest? Once the mold has grown on the bread, look at it while the bread is still in the bag. Please throw it out once you have looked at it. **Remember, never eat moldy bread!**

CHAPTER 3
MICROBES IN WATER

We've seen how microbes can both help and hurt us in our bodies. Now let's take a look at how they both help and hurt the ecosystems in bodies of water.

Have you ever heard the phrase "safety in numbers?" This means that it's easier to survive as part of a group than alone. Bacteria do not often grow as a single colony in nature. Instead, they come together and form a large sheet of bacteria called a biofilm. Do you remember that bacteria form biofilms in our mouth as well?

? **ESSENTIAL QUESTION**

Why are microbes an important part of aquatic ecosystems?

An individual bacterium gains many advantages by becoming part of a biofilm. It can communicate with nearby bacteria, obtain new genetic material, stay in an area with plenty of nutrients, and enjoy better protection.

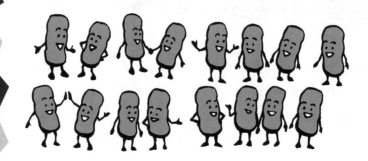

When a biofilm becomes several layers thick, it's called a **microbial mat**. Biofilms and microbial mats can contain several different types of bacteria. You can find them in water and on land.

• • • • • FRESHWATER ENVIRONMENTS • • • • •

Lakes, ponds, streams, and rivers are **freshwater** environments. If you swim in a pond, do your lips taste salty afterward? Most freshwater systems contain water with very little salt. Microbes play an important role in freshwater ecosystems.

What happens to ponds during the winter in cold areas? Ponds in cooler areas tend to freeze over in winter. If you live in a hotter area with very little rain, **evaporation** causes ponds and lakes to lose water. This happens more in times of **drought**. The truth is, all ponds and lakes are constantly changing in ways that we cannot see!

Think of ponds and lakes as having layers. The top layer has a lot of oxygen. This is where microbes that like an aerobic environment hang out. Protists, such as algae and diatoms, and aerobic bacteria, such as cyanobacteria, live in this layer.

Since this layer also gets the most sunlight, these microbes use photosynthesis to generate energy and produce oxygen and organic matter. The microbes become part of the aquatic **food web** when other aquatic organisms, such as plankton and fish, breathe the oxygen and eat the organic matter.

The middle layer has fewer algae, cyanobacteria, and diatoms than the top layer. It also has less oxygen and stays cool for most of the year. Can you figure out why? The bottom layer has little to

no oxygen—it's an anaerobic environment. What kinds of microbes like to grow here?

Organic matter not used by the top and middle layer drops to the bottom, like leaves drop to a forest floor. Anaerobic bacteria break down that organic matter. The process of decomposition produces carbon dioxide gas that other organisms, such as plants, can use.

51

OILY ALGAE!

Did you know that gasoline comes from microbes? Crude oil is converted from algae deep underground—but it takes a million years to make. Today, scientists have found a way to convert algae to crude oil in only an hour. Now that is slick! How do they do this? First, scientists select algae strains that make a lot of oil. The oil has to be **extracted** from the algae before it can be made into something that will be sold at a gas station. Scientists grow a large batch of algae and use either chemicals, a hydraulic press, or a combination of high heat and high pressure to remove the oil from inside the algae's cells. The product you get is a green slurry that is chemically similar to the **fossil fuels** that oil companies find underground. No need to wait a million years! You can watch a video of the process scientists use to turn a sample of algae into crude oil!

algae crude oil Truthloader 🔍

WORDS TO KNOW

extract: to remove something.

fossil fuels: oil, natural gas, and coal, which are natural fuels that formed long ago from the remains of living organisms.

• • • BALANCING ACT • • •

Just as your body wants to keep a balance among microbes, an aquatic ecosystem needs to maintain a balance between microbes, oxygen, nutrients, and organisms. All of these things are interconnected, which means changes in one part of the system cause changes in the other parts.

If there are fewer nutrients in the water, there will be fewer microbes.

WORDS TO KNOW

sewage: waste from buildings, carried away through sewers. A sewer is a drain for waste.

consumption: using something.

compensate: to do something positive to counter a negative effect.

Freshwater microbes face small daily changes, but sometimes the balance is completely thrown off when a big, unexpected change happens. For example, a spill of **sewage** into a river might empty into a lake, bringing new organic matter that pollutes the lake and alters the ecosystem. The recovery from pollution to health can be long.

Scientists can measure how well a lake or pond is recovering by testing oxygen use or measuring organic waste **consumption**.

Did You Know?

Dumping organic sewage into a pond or lake can cause the water to turn bright green! Algae, cyanobacteria, and aquatic plants become so overgrown that the water appears green. Then the water can't be used by animals who depend on it to survive.

••SALTWATER ENVIRONMENTS••

Saltwater ecosystems are very different from freshwater ecosystems. Oceans generally contain fewer nutrients for microbes than ponds do, except in areas close to land. To **compensate** for having less food available, microbes are smaller and fewer in number. Why do you think microbes that live where there are fewer nutrients are smaller?

53

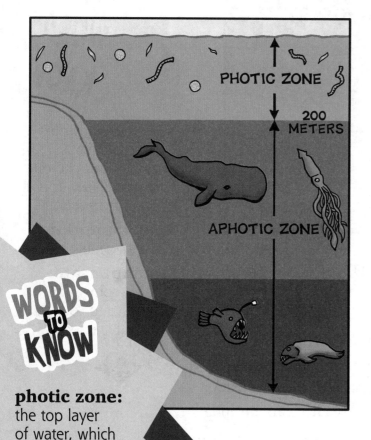

PHOTIC ZONE

200 METERS

APHOTIC ZONE

Bacteria prefer to live in the upper tier of the ocean, called the **photic zone**. Several bacteria are active in the photic zone, including one that is closely related to the cyanobacteria. It is called a *Prochlorococcus* and can use photosynthesis to make food and consume organic matter.

The deeper down you go in an ocean, the fewer bacteria you find. Can you imagine what it would look and feel like on the ocean floor? The ocean can go down to depths of greater than 30,000 feet!

If you were a microbe, it might not be the best place to live. It is a dark, cold, high-pressure environment with very little food available.

Few bacteria and archaea can live in such conditions. Most prefer a warmer area. Thermophilic archaea live at hot hydrothermal vents found deep in the ocean. Thermophiles can live in these vents because they need hot temperatures to grow.

WORDS TO KNOW

photic zone: the top layer of water, which receives the most sunlight.

marine: found in the ocean.

Did You Know?

Marine microbes are responsible for generating half of the nutrients available for the oceanic food web! Want to see some interesting marine microbes? Head over to *National Geographic's* gallery of marine microbes!

National Geographic image marine microbes

Bacteria and algae live in the open ocean, but definitely prefer coastal areas. Coastal areas have shallow zones where microbes find more nutrients than they do in the open ocean. More nutrients mean more microbes! A larger population of microbes allows for more aquatic organisms, such as fish and crabs.

If you were a microbe, where would you prefer to live? In the open ocean, coastal area, or in a lake? Why?

WORDS TO KNOW

bioremediation: the process of using biological organisms to clean up a polluted area.

MICROBES TO THE RESCUE!

Have you ever heard of an oil tanker spilling oil in the ocean? Luckily, microbes can come to the rescue to help clean the spill. In a process called **bioremediation**, microbes such as bacteria, fungi, and a few protists change the oil into carbon dioxide. The process is slow and complex. Unfortunately, the microbes cannot always clean up the entire oil spill, which leaves many marine mammals and organisms vulnerable to the dangerous effects of the oil. You can watch a video of bioremediation.

microbe oil spill clean up 🔍

55

GLOBAL WARMING

Global warming has the effect of increasing the average temperatures on Earth. An increase of just a degree or two in the average temperature of the atmosphere has been shown to be enough to melt glaciers and the polar ice caps, raising the level of the oceans. Greenhouse gases are directly responsible for global warming.

Carbon dioxide is a greenhouse gas released into the atmosphere from burning fossil fuels. How do carbon dioxide and other greenhouse gases increase the temperature on Earth? By trapping heat in the atmosphere like a blanket.

The oceans absorb carbon dioxide from the atmosphere. While this helps to reduce the level of carbon dioxide in the atmosphere, carbon dioxide is hurting the ecosystems in the ocean as well! It makes the ocean more acidic, which makes it hard for crustaceans, corals, and mollusks to make their shells and skeletons.

If you change one part of an ecosystem, what do you think happens to other members of the ecosystem? Do you think microbes will become affected? Do you think that microbes can help change this situation?

scientists microbes methane 🔍

Now we know that microbes are an important part of our ecosystems and that they sometimes can even fix our damaged aquatic environments. Can you think of other ways that microbes can help sustain and fix our aquatic ecosystems?

? ESSENTIAL QUESTION

Now it's time to consider and discuss the Essential Question:
Why are microbes an important part of aquatic ecosystems?

GROW, ALGAE, GROW!

IDEAS FOR SUPPLIES

gallon-sized plastic bags ✳ lichen ✳ soil ✳ liquid plant food

Algae use photosynthesis to grow. Will plant food help algae grow?

1 Ask an adult to take you to a pond or lake. Use a plastic bottle to collect about 2 cups of water. At home, put 1 cup of pond water into each of two separate bags.

2 Lichen is part of the Fungi Kingdom and has algae or cyanobacteria inside. It often grows on tree bark or rocks. Find some lichen and scrape off about 1 tablespoon into a bag with tap water.

3 Dig 1 tablespoon of dirt from an area that has plenty of access to sunlight. Put this into a bag with 1 cup of tap water.

4 Put 5 drops of liquid plant food into each of the bags with dirt and lichen and one of the bags with pond water. Add a few rocks for the algae to stick to. Get the excess air out of the bags while sealing. Label each with its contents and place them in a warm area with sunlight.

5 Record your experiment in a scientific method worksheet. What is your hypothesis? Where will the algae grow? Check your bags every few days and record your observations. Does the plant food help the algae grow?

THINK MORE: What other areas in your environment might contain algae? Take a sample and run an experiment! Change the experimental conditions. Do you think algae will grow if it is kept in the dark?

BRRR, THAT'S COLD!

IDEAS FOR SUPPLIES
4 prepared media containers ✳ *plastic wrap* ✳ *incubator* ✳ *several swabs*

The temperature of the deep ocean is about 32 degrees Fahrenheit (0 degrees Celsius), about the same as your refrigerator! Not many bacteria like to live in such a cold temperature. You can use your refrigerator to see how some bacteria grow in the cold and how they might live in the deep ocean.

1 While the media plates warm to room temperature, wash your hands. While you can't create a sterile environment, keeping your hands clean will help you get good results.

2 Prepare two negative controls labeled *negative control incubator* and *negative control refrigerator*. Remove the lids, cover the tops with plastic wrap, and secure with a rubber band. Put one negative control in the incubator and one in the refrigerator upside down.

3 With a damp swab, swab different areas in your house, including doorknobs, the sink, and under the faucets. Choose two new media plates and gently swipe the swab back and forth over the entire surfaces on both plates. Do not push the swab into the media.

4 Cover both containers with plastic wrap, label one *household incubator* and one *household refrigerator*. Put one in the incubator and one in the refrigerator upside down.

5 Record your experiment in your science journal. What is your hypothesis? Which plates will have microbes growing on them?

6 Look at your plates, but don't unwrap them. Record your results at 24, 48, and 72 hours. Write down how many colonies you see and describe those colonies. Are there differences in microbial growth in the containers from the refrigerator versus those from the incubator? Are there differences in the size of the colonies?

THINK MORE: What do you think would happen if you repeated the experiment with some changes. You could remove all containers from the refrigerator after 24 hours and put them in the incubator. Would this change your results? Why or why not?

WORDS TO KNOW

biofuel: fuel made from living matter, such as plants.

MICROBES TO THE RESCUE . . . AGAIN?

By using algae to make **biofuel**, we can also reduce the amount of carbon dioxide in the air. This is because algae use carbon dioxide in photosynthesis. Wouldn't it be cool if we could use algae to create fuel for energy, while at the same time cleaning extra carbon dioxide from the atmosphere and the oceans? Can microbes help us to stop using fossil fuels and slow global warming?

MAKE A WINOGRADSKY COLUMN

IDEAS FOR SUPPLIES

2 clean, empty plastic bottles ✳ 2 buckets or large containers ✳ gloves ✳ plastic wrap ✳ 1 egg yolk (separate from egg white) ✳ finely shredded newspaper

Dr. Sergei Winogradsky was a Russian scientist who loved to observe microbial growth and interactions in aquatic and soil habitats. You can set up your own aquatic habitat and see if you can find different populations of microbes. The egg yolk provides sulfur that can be used by anaerobic microbes, such as purple sulfur and green sulfur bacteria, to grow. This experiment will take six to eight weeks to complete.

1 Ask an adult to cut off the top parts of each bottle, right where the bottle begins to taper off. Keep the bottom part of the bottles and discard the top portions. The bottles are for your columns.

2 Visit your favorite pond. At the edge of the water, dig as deep as you can below the water surface and collect 5 cups of pond mud in the first bucket. Collect 3 cups of pond water in the second bucket.

3 At home, put on gloves and remove any sticks, stones, leaves, and other large debris from the pond mud.

4 To prepare the control column, fill one bottle three-quarters full with pond mud. Firmly pack the mud and tap the bottle against a counter to release any air bubbles. Why do we not want air bubbles in the column? Add ¼ cup of pond water on top of the mud. Cover with plastic wrap and label the bottle *control* with the date.

5 To prepare the experimental column, combine an egg yolk and finely shredded newspaper. Add to the remaining mud. Fill the second bottle with the mud-yolk-newspaper mixture just as you did the control. Label the bottle *experimental* with the date. Add ¼ cup of pond water to the top of the experimental column. Cover with plastic wrap.

6 Place both bottles in a warm area that receives some natural light. Record your experiment in your science journal. What is your hypothesis?

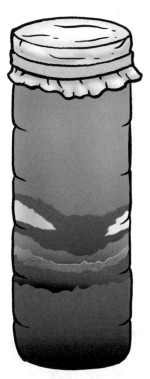

7 Check your columns at least once a week and write down what you see. Taking a picture of your columns each week is helpful, because you will see many changes over the course of the experiment. Have certain areas changed color? Are there distinctive sheets of microbes? Where are the aerobic bacteria growing? Where are the anaerobic bacteria growing?

THINK MORE: Would the Winogradsky column change if you put the bottle in an area with no light? What else could you add to the experimental column?

61

CULTURE WINOGRADSKY COLUMN BACTERIA

IDEAS FOR SUPPLIES
4 media plates ✳ *Winogradsky columns from previous project* ✳ *incubator*

Let's get a closer look at the bacteria in your Winogradsky columns by culturing them on media plates in your incubator.

1 If your media plates were stored in the refrigerator, let them warm up for 1 hour at room temperature. **Don't forget to wash your hands!**

2 Prepare and label your negative control as you have done before and place it in the incubator upside down.

3 Culture aerobic microbes by swabbing an area with microbial growth near the top of your control Winogradsky column. Gently swipe the swab over the entire surface of a clean media plate. Cover the container with plastic wrap, label it *aerobic #1*, and place it in the incubator upside down.

4 Repeat step 3 with two different places in your experimental Winogradsky column.

5 What is your hypothesis? Start a scientific method worksheet to organize your experiment.

6 Look at your plates, but don't unwrap them. Record your results at 24, 48, and 72 hours. Write down how many colonies you get, and details about the colonies.

THINK MORE: Which Winogradsky column produced the most bacteria? Why do you think this happened?

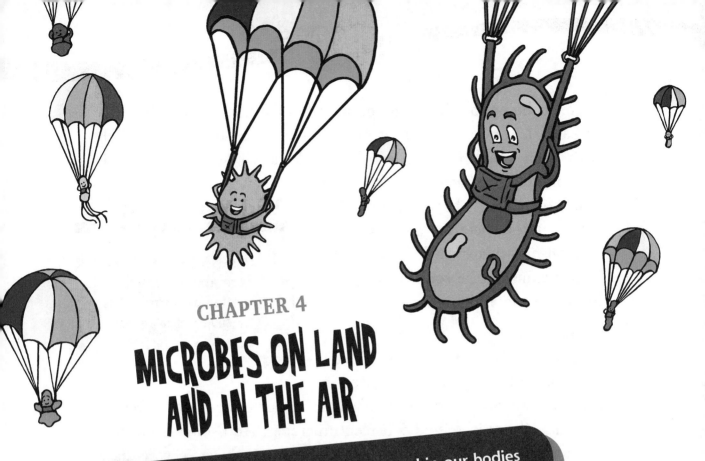

CHAPTER 4
MICROBES ON LAND AND IN THE AIR

We've learned that microbes can be found in our bodies and in our water. It probably won't surprise you to learn that you can also find microbes in the soil and in the air!

• • • • • • • • DIGGING IN THE DIRT • • • • • • • •

Go outside and pick up a handful of soil. What do you see? Dirt, rocks, grass, and maybe an ant or a worm? That handful of soil also contains something you can't see. In fact, it contains about 10 billion things you can't see!

You're probably holding about 10 billion microbes that make their habitat in the ground! Soil is much more complex than just the dirt that we see.

? ESSENTIAL QUESTION

What purpose do microbes serve in soil and in the air?

63

Soil is home to a bustling community of fungi, protists, bacteria, archaea, and viruses. Soil is where microbial communities fight with each other for nutrients and where viruses infect certain communities of bacteria. Among all that competition between microbial communities, there are also symbiotic relationships. Can you believe all this is happening in the soil that you have in your hand right now?

There are different types of soil particles in your handful of dirt. Sand is the largest soil particle, followed by silt and clay. Soil is made up of about 50 percent air and water, 45 percent soil particles, and 5 percent microbes. Add some organisms, organic matter, minerals, and salts, and you have a very basic ecosystem!

Did You Know?

Scientists believe there are about 30,000 varieties of microbes in any given area of soil.

SOIL COMPOSITION

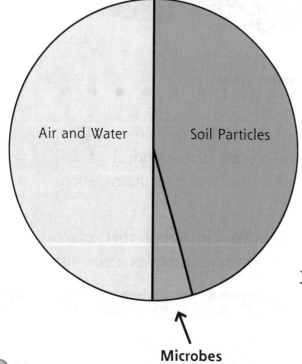

Air and Water

Soil Particles

Microbes

Microbes in the soil are important to plants.

They provide plants with food and energy in a form the plant can use and, in turn, plants provide microbes with organic matter. Large communities of microbes surround plant roots. The farther away you move from plant roots, the fewer microbes you will find.

Many relationships between microbes and plants are symbiotic and friendly. One such relationship can be found between a unique group of bacteria called **rhizobia** and a group of plants called **legumes**. Rhizobia live in **nodules** formed on the roots of legume plants, where they help legumes get the nutrients they need.

WORDS TO KNOW

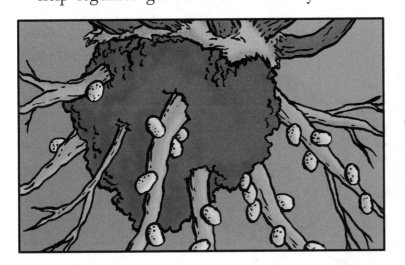

rhizobia: special bacteria that live in nodules growing off a legume's plant root.

legume: a plant with seeds that grow in pods, such as peas and beans.

nodule: a small rounded swelling.

nitrogen fixation: the process of turning nitrogen gas into a liquid.

Plants need nitrogen in the same way humans need oxygen, but they can't use nitrogen in gas form. The rhizobia change nitrogen gas into liquid ammonia, which other bacteria convert into a form of nitrogen the plant can use. The process of turning nitrogen gas into a liquid is called **nitrogen fixation**. Ammonia can be turned into nitrite, and nitrite to nitrate, which the plant can use.

In return, plants give the bacteria protection in the rhizobia, as well as simple organic compounds, such as sugars, that they can use to grow. If you would like to see some rhizobia, all you have to do is grow some pea plants and look at the roots.

Fixation usually happens through microbes, but it can also happen in the air as a result of a lightning strike!

carnivorous: a plant or animal that eats meat. Some plants trap and digest small animals, mostly insects.

Carnivorous plants also benefit from the presence of microbes. Unlike most plants, carnivorous plants eat mostly insects. They are similar to other plants in that they also need nitrogen and cannot make it themselves. They often live in nitrogen-poor areas, so what do they rely on? Microbes!

A diverse community of algae, bacteria, fungi, and other organisms live within the plant. These microbes digest any insect that comes their way to make nitrogen available to the plant in a solid form it can use.

I'M "LICHEN" THE WAY YOU GROW!

Have you ever see lichen growing on a tree? Lichen is composed of a fungus combined with either a cyanobacterium or an algae. The algae or cyanobacterium uses photosynthesis to make sugars for the fungus to grow, while the fungus protects the algae or cyanobacterium. The tree provides the lichen with water and a place to grow. The lichen occasionally supplies the tree with a source of nitrogen, but mostly it just grows on the tree in a way that doesn't cause damage. You can watch a video about lichen. Why do you think we know so little about lichen?

hunting wild lichen

Fungi are also beneficial to plants and trees. Fungi provide plants with a mineral called phosphorus that plants need to thrive. In exchange, the plants gives the fungi sugars and other useful substances that the fungi need to grow.

Microbes don't just help plants growing in soil get the nitrogen they need to grow. They help in other ways, too. Protists, fungi, and bacteria all help to decompose organic matter into nutrients that plants, trees, insects, and animals can use. Organisms die, leaves fall, and organic waste is left behind. What would the forests be like if there was no one to remove these items? We wouldn't be able to walk in the woods because it would be filled with mountains of leaves!

Did You Know?

Decomposers, such as dung beetles and earthworms, are the trash collectors of the natural world!

You can learn more about them in this short video.

decomposers NOVA 🔍

Fungi and bacteria uphold the circle of life. Organisms live, then die, then get recycled by fungi and bacteria into nutrients that can be used to help support new life.

Fungi and bacteria decompose organic matter, such as cellulose and proteins, by digesting and making it into simple forms that can be used by other microbes. Worms also eat organic matter, but they have microbes in their guts that help them digest it.

Microbes are present in soil and water, but what about in the air? Try shaking out a rag or pillowcase in the sunlight. What do you see? If you had a high-powered microscope, you could see microbes catching rides on those dust particles. Fungi, bacteria, and viruses can be found on dust, soil, and water droplets.

Microbes can't fly, but they can ride on a water droplet, a particle of dust, or a soil particle.

Put your hand in front of your mouth and breathe in and out for a few minutes. What does your hand feel like? When we breathe out, we release very tiny droplets into the air with microbes hanging onto them. When we breathe in, tiny droplets with microbes enter our noses and mouths and eventually reach our lungs.

When we sneeze, we release a lot of saliva and microbes into the air at once. That's why you should sneeze into a tissue, even if you aren't sick.

Did You Know?

Not all relationships between plants and microbes are good ones. Some microbes are pathogens of plants. Like humans and other animals, plants have an immune system to defend themselves against microbial intruders.

IT'S A BIRD, IT'S A PLANE, IT'S A MICROBE!

In 2006, a scientific study looked at the number of different microbes found in the air in two cities in Texas during a period of 17 weeks. The genetic test they used was only able to test for the presence of bacteria and archaea. We might not think that being in the air is a great place for microbes to exist given that air is dry and devoid of a lot of nutrients. But these scientists found a startling number of microbes present—2,000 different types of bacteria or archaeans at any given time! That certainly is a lot of microbes to breathe in and out of our mouths and lungs every day.

Not only does air contain a lot of living microbes, but a recent study has shown that air can transport microbes thousands of miles. The Sahara Desert in Africa produces millions of tons of dust each year, and the microbes within it have been found in the southeastern United States.

Microbes can also be found on non-living objects.

A non-living object that has the potential to carry microbes is called a **fomite**. Look around your room. How many fomites do you see? Which fomites are likely to have a lot of microbes on them? Which fomite is more likely to have microbes on it, one that is cleaned more often or less often?

WORDS TO KNOW

fomite: a non-living object that can have microbes on it.

• • • • • • • MICROBES IN SPACE! • • • • • • •

Remember biofilms and microbial mats from Chapter 3? NASA has been studying microbial mats on Earth for quite a while. Microbial mats are self-sufficient collections of microbes where different layers produce products that are food for microbes in another layer.

Many fossils have been found to show that microbial mats existed at least 350 million years ago. NASA believes that these ancient microbes offer clues about what to look for when searching for evidence of life on other planets. In fact, a recent scientific paper suggests that there are structures that look like microbial mats on other planets.

Did You Know?

There are fewer microbes in the air outside than inside a house. This is a good reason to open the windows in your house every day to let in some fresh air!

If this turns out to be true, then Mars might have supported life at one time.

We have looked at what microbes are doing in the ground, discussed their existence in the air, and even considered their potential to be in space! Right now, we know that microbes in the ground are often living in symbiotic relationships with surrounding organisms. Certainly, microbes exist in the air and can often be carried thousands of miles.

Science is forging onward as we continue to ask questions about the world around us, but many questions still do not have answers. For example, are microbes in the air only temporarily, as a way to move to a new area? Is there some long-term advantage to being carried in the air for thousands of miles? Can you think of any other questions?

? ESSENTIAL QUESTION

Now it's time to consider and discuss the Essential Question: What purpose do microbes serve in soil and in the air?

HOW CLEAN IS YOUR AIR?

Lichens are often used as monitors of air quality. There are three main types of lichen: crustose looks flat and crusty, foliose looks leafy, and fruticose looks bushy. If you can't find any lichens growing in an area, that's a sign of heavy air pollution. If you only spot crustose lichen, there is moderate air pollution. If you can find foliose lichen and crustose lichen, there is little or no air pollution. If you find foliose, crustose, and fruticose lichen, you have found an area with clean air!

1 In your back yard, find as many lichen as you can. Look on the ground, on rocks, and on trees. Record which types you can find—crustose, foliose, or fruticose. Make drawings of each in your science journal.

2 Based on the types of lichen that you have found, make a hypothesis of how clean the air is.

3 Go to a park or other wooded area and follow the same procedure as in step 1. Do you live in a big city? Can you find lichen? What kinds?

THINK MORE: Where would you expect to find more types of lichen, in the countryside or in a city?

  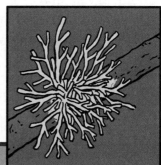

MAKE YOUR OWN COMPOST

IDEAS FOR SUPPLIES

2 pieces of wood, approximately 12 inches by 4 inches by 3 inches ✳ *2 plastic containers with lids (22- and 20-gallon)* ✳ *knife* ✳ *fine mesh (12 inches by 12 inches)* ✳ *duct tape* ✳ *soil* ✳ *worms* ✳ *newspaper* ✳ *leaves and grass clippings*

Safety Tip: Ask an adult to help you with the knife.

Compost provides a great opportunity to see microbes in action! With a composting box, you can see decomposition on a daily basis.

1 To make the compost bin, place the wood pieces on the bottom of the 22-gallon container, spaced equally apart. Ask an adult to poke holes in the bottom of the smaller container. Put the smaller container inside the larger one on top of the wood pieces. Worms can't live in dirt that's too wet—that's why you see them on driveways and roads after it's rained a lot. Why is it important to make your compost bin capable of draining?

2 Ask an adult to cut a 6-inch-by-6-inch square hole into one container lid. Turn the lid over, and place the mesh over the square hole and tape it in place with duct tape. This will let air into the compost bin and keep insects, such as flies, out of the bin.

Did You Know?

Newspaper strips add carbon to the compost and coffee grounds provide roughage for the worms.

3 Time to fill your compost bin! Add slightly moist soil and worms on the bottom. Layer newspaper strips, leaves, grass clippings, vegetable and fruit peelings, and coffee grounds. **Never add meat, dairy, or citrus to your compost bin.**

4 Check on your bin every few days. It might smell unpleasant at first, but after a few weeks it will smell just like dirt. Drain any excess water from the bottom container.

5 Check on your worms periodically by putting on gloves and mixing the contents of the compost bin. Do you see more worms than you put in? If moisture has collected in the bottom of the outer container, you might be able to see worm eggs. They are white and smaller than a grain of rice. Keep these eggs and put them back into your ecosystem or put them in a flower patch.

THINK MORE: What kind of microbes do you think are in your contained ecosystem? Grow some on prepared media plates. Are there differences between the microbes at the top of the pile and those in the bottom of the pile? How many colonies do you get and what do you notice about them?

YEAST ALL AROUND US!

IDEAS FOR SUPPLIES
unbleached flour ✳ *bottled water filtered with a carbon filter*

**There are many thousands of microbes in the
air at any one time. Let's find some!**

1 Pour 1 cup of flour and ½ cup of bottled water into a glass mixing bowl. Mix well with a spoon so the mixture looks like thick oatmeal. Cover the glass container with plastic wrap and keep in a warm place in your house overnight.

2 Start a scientific method worksheet to record your experiment in your science journal. You will be making daily observations.

3 After 24 hours, check the flour-water mixture. Do you see any bubbles? If not, don't worry, continue with the next step.

4 Remove half of the flour-water mixture and throw it away. Add a new cup of flour and ½ cup of water to the remaining mixture in the glass container and combine well with a spoon. Cover this with plastic wrap and place in a warm spot in the house for 24 hours.

5 Check the mixture. Do you see any bubbles? If so, that's proof of something living in your mixture—yeast! Some yeast came from the air and some came from the flour. You have made what is called a "starter" yeast mixture!

6 If you would like to bake bread with your starter yeast, you need to feed it twice a day for a week before you can use it. To feed your yeast starter, first take ½ of the yeast mixture and throw it away. Then add one cup of all purpose, unbleached flour and ½ cup of bottled water to the remaining yeast mixture. Do this about every 12 hours.

Did You Know?

Soil microbes are everywhere on Earth except in active volcanoes.

7 Check the smell of the yeast mixture every time you feed it. It should have a pleasant, slightly tangy aroma. If it smells awful, something has gone wrong. Throw out the starter mixture and start all over again. If it passes the smell test and you have fed your yeast starter mixture for one week, you are ready to use your starter mixture to bake some bread!

8 Go tokingarthurflour.com/recipes/rustic-sourdough-bread-recipe for a sourdough recipe using the starter you just made! **Ask an adult to help you bake a loaf of bread.** Happy baking!

THINK MORE: Why are we using non-chlorinated bottled water with our yeast mixture instead of tap water? Why are we using unbleached flour with our yeast mixture instead of bleached flour?

FUN WITH FOMITES

IDEAS FOR SUPPLIES
3 prepared media plates ✳ *cotton swabs* ✳ *plastic wrap* ✳ *rubber band*

Now that you've learned about microbes in your environment, let's check out some fomites and see what's on them.

1 Make your control media plate as described in previous projects and place it upside down in the incubator. Wash your hands.

2 Now take a cotton swab, wet it with a little bit of water and pick a doorknob that is used often by your family. Make sure to swipe all around the doorknob with your cotton swab for a good 10 seconds.

3 Carefully take the cotton swab and choose a new media plate. Gently place the swab on the surface of the media and swipe it back and forth over the entire surface. Do not push the swab into the media too hard or some gelatin will break off. Throw the swab away  into the garbage. Cover the container with plastic wrap and a rubber band. Now label a piece of masking tape with _____ doorknob. Put this in the incubator upside down as well. If you have a heat wrap, now is a good time to put it in the incubator.

4 Repeat step 3 with a new swab and a different doorknob. Choose a doorknob that is used much less or has been recently cleaned. Prepare a new container and label this one as _____ doorknob.

5 Start a scientific method worksheet in your science journal. What is your hypothesis? What kind of microbes do you think will grow and on which plates will they grow?

6 Look at your plates, but don't unwrap them. Record your results at 24, 48, and 72 hours. Write down how many colonies you got and details about the colonies themselves. Are they smooth or wrinkled? What color are they?

THINK MORE: Can you think of other areas in your house that might serve as fomites? If you repeat the experiment, do the microbes look different or the same?

MICROBES ON THE SUBWAY

In 2014, scientists decided to discover what types of microbes were present in the New York City subway system. They swabbed many different fomites, including ticket booths, turnstiles, benches, and seats and found more than 500 species of bacteria! Most of the bacteria are harmless, but some of them are capable of causing illnesses. Microbes also love to travel in trains, buses, and planes as well! Read an article about microbes on the subway and view a map of New York City pathogens.

pathogen map 🔍

bacteria fungi ride dust 🔍

CHAPTER 5

PATHOGENS: MICROBES ON THE DARK SIDE

We have learned that some microbes can be helpful and some can be harmful. Harmful microbes are called pathogens. They can cause diseases in people, animals, plants, or other microbes. When a pathogen infects a host and makes it sick, the pathogen benefits. But the host usually feels terrible!

If a microbe is a virus, then we know it's a pathogen and it's going to be harmful. The bacterial, fungal, and protist groups have both symbionts and pathogens. So far the archaeans are the only microbial group found to have only helpful organisms. That could always change, though. There may be an archaean pathogen just waiting to be found by an adventurous scientist.

? ESSENTIAL QUESTION

How do scientists know that microbes cause illnesses?

Each pathogen infects a host in a different way.

For example, viruses need to enter host cells and use them to make more viruses. Then they leave to start the process all over again inside new host cells. Bacteria infect hosts in several ways. Like viruses, a few bacteria need to infect a host cell. But most bacteria do not need to be inside a host cell to cause an infection—they can cause an infection outside of a cell.

While fungi will also cause an infection outside of a cell, protists can cause an infection inside or outside of the cell, depending on the pathogen. These are some interesting facts, but how did scientists figure out that microbes existed and what illnesses they cause?

Did You Know?

There are more marine viruses than marine bacteria in the ocean! These viruses only infect bacteria and archaea.

• • • • • DISCOVERING PATHOGENS • • • • •

Hundreds of years ago, there were no microscopes to see microbes. Scientists had to use their powers of observation and imagination. Many scientists and doctors made observations about the causes of illness. In 1546, Dr. Girolamo Fracastoro, a physician in Italy, first described pathogenic microbes as contagions. He defined a contagion as an unseen particle that could pass infection from one living thing to another.

By observing his patients, Dr. Fracastoro noticed that there were several ways to get infected. These included passing the contagion from a sick person directly to a healthy person or from an object that an infected person had touched.

Today, we all know that a sick person is infected with a microbe. We try to stay away from them or at least wash our hands if we come in contact with them or something they have touched. It took a long time for scientists and the medical community to realize that hand washing could help prevent the spread of microbes. We'll discuss hand washing in the next section.

It took 100 years after Dr. Fracastoro's observations before scientists would actually see contagions. In the 1600s, Robert Hooke and Antonie van Leeuwenhoek developed hand-held microscopes that allowed them to see microbes. Hooke and van Leeuwenhoek provided detailed illustrations that captivated people's interest in these tiny living things.

Once microbes were visible they were found in all sorts of places!

As scientific tools and techniques continued to evolve, more questions could be asked and answered. Which microbes caused which infections? Luckily, we don't have to worry about this today. Your physician knows which microbes cause which infections, but in the 1800s, this was not completely understood.

DR. LOUIS PASTEUR

WORDS TO KNOW

sterilize: to make clean and free of any microbes.

Remember Dr. Louis Pasteur, the young chemist from France, who we met briefly in the Introduction? Even though people knew about the existence of microbes and could see them, there was still much that was unknown about microbes. For example, where did microbes come from? Some scientists believed that they appeared out of nowhere to make people sick or food rotten.

Dr. Pasteur devised elegant experiments to prove that microbes could only arise from other microbes. He put a yeast infusion into a glass flask and bent the neck of the flask into an S-shape. He boiled the yeast infusion to force all the air out of the flask and **sterilize** the contents.

Even after several days, he observed no microbial growth in the flask. The microbes in the infusion died during boiling so that no new ones could arise. The S shape of the flask kept dust particles with new microbes out of the infusion. This was an important finding to show that microbes didn't just magically appear out of nothing.

Did You Know?

PS

You can see Dr. Pasteur's original sketches of his experiments. Can you see why it is so important for scientists to record and keep all their observations?

LOC recherches generations 🔍

Dr. Robert Koch, a German physician and bacteriologist, developed rules that helped determine which infection is caused by which microbe. These rules, called postulates, were written in 1876. They have shaped much of the modern medicine we use today.

Microbial Postulates by Dr. Robert Koch	
1.	The microbe must be present in all patients with the same infection.
2.	The microbe must be isolated from each sick patient in a pure culture. This means that under sterile conditions, only one type of microbe should grow from the patient sample. If you have different types of microbes growing, then you don't know which microbe is responsible for the infection.
3.	The microbe from the pure culture must cause the same infection when introduced to a different, healthy individual.
4.	The microbe must be re-isolated from the patient in postulate #3 and the pure culture must yield the exact same microbe that infected this patient in postulate #1. Again, this is proof that a certain microbe causes a certain infection.

These postulates describe the exact steps a scientist or physician must take to ensure that a certain microbe causes a certain disease. With these guidelines in place, many new research studies could begin to characterize microbes.

There is still a lot of research on different microbes under way. Scientists are trying to figure out how each pathogen causes illness and exactly what steps are involved during the infection.

The ultimate goal of studying each infection is to prevent it or to at least find a cure for the illness.

This is not easy to do! Usually, different groups of scientists tackle different parts of the infection. For example, there are scientists studying the Ebola virus right now. Some groups are trying to understand what steps the virus uses to get inside a cell. A different group of researchers is trying to make a medicine to block the steps of infection. Other scientists are trying to design a vaccine against Ebola. All of these groups are working to **eradicate** Ebola.

WORDS TO KNOW

eradicate: to get rid of forever.

outbreak: an expected seasonal rise in the number of infections in one area.

KNOW YOUR MICROBES

EBOLA VIRUS

Viral Pathogen • Infects people and several animals, including bats and monkeys

Claim to fame: Caused an epidemic in 2014 and several **outbreaks** before that

• • • • • WASH THOSE HANDS! • • • • •

Dr. Fracastoro's observations showed that contagions could spread from person to person or from an object to a person. Unfortunately, these observations did not lead to the use of hand washing to control the spread of pathogens. That idea would only arrive several hundred years later!

In 1850, Dr. Ignaz Semmelweis was a physician in an Austrian hospital. He noticed that patients in the physician and medical student sections of the hospital were more likely to get infections after surgery than those patients housed in the midwives' sections.

He also noticed something else. Physicians and medical students, but not midwives, would routinely move from working on a corpse to doing a surgery on a living patient without washing their hands.

Dr. Semmelweis connected the dots and realized that, by not washing their hands, physicians and medical students were probably giving infections to their patients. He desperately tried to get medical staff to wash their hands before doing any surgery in a hospital setting.

Did You Know?

In the 1800s, aside from proving that microbes could only come from other microbes, Dr. Pasteur also showed that heat and certain chemicals could "kill" and prevent microbes from growing.

Members of the medical community rejected the recommendation to wash their hands before doing a surgery. They were even offended by it.

From the physicians' point of view, it seemed that Dr. Semmelweis was saying that doctors were infecting their patients on purpose. Dr. Semmelweis did not help himself by publicly outing members of the medical community. His hand-washing idea and behavior got him in such hot water that he was eventually committed to an asylum for people with mental illness, where he died at age 47. Although Dr. Semmelweis was unable to influence the medical community, he did set the stage for future scientists to continue his work.

At this point, it was understood that sick people had microbes on them. Armed with the knowledge of Dr. Pasteur's experiments and Dr. Semmelweis' observations, a physician from England named Dr. Joseph Lister performed his own experiments. He tested **carbolic acid** on instruments used in surgeries and on human skin. He successfully prevented an infection in a young boy's wound by dipping a piece of cotton in carbolic acid and applying it to the wound.

KNOW YOUR MICROBES

MERS VIRUS (CORONAVIRUS)

Also known as Middle Eastern respiratory syndrome

Viral Pathogen • Infects people and animals, including camels

Claim to fame: Respiratory illness that often kills its victims; seen in 2012 in the Middle East

WORDS TO KNOW

carbolic acid: a powerful antimicrobial and disinfectant.

antiseptic: using clean and sterile methods to do any microbiological procedure.

Dr. Lister published his findings in a medical journal, and before long the medical community realized the importance of hand washing and **antiseptic** techniques. What do you think carbolic acid did to a wound? What effect would carbolic acid have on any microbes in the wound?

85

• • • • • • A TRIP TO THE DOCTOR • • • • • •

If you are sick, you want to get better as quickly as possible. How do you do that? You go to your doctor! But how do physicians figure out what you are infected with so that they can prescribe the right medicine?

Doctors want to match up a person's illness with the medicine that will work best. To do this, they need to know what pathogen is causing the infection. There are a few steps doctors take to make sure they know which pathogen they are dealing with.

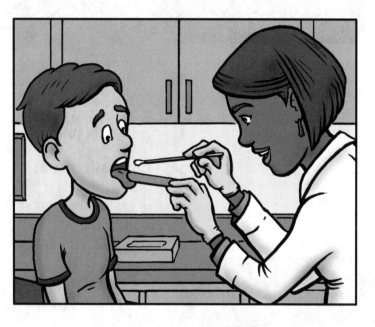

Several different microbes can cause illnesses with similar symptoms.

Even though a doctor may guess which microbe the patient is sick with, they will want to make sure so the patient gets the correct medicine. Different medicines work on different microbes. A medicine might kill one bacterium, but not another. If the medicine does not kill the bacterium the patient is infected with, the patient will stay sick.

To make sure the patient is treated with the right medicine, the physician will take a sample from the area that is red and swollen. For example, if the patient has a sore throat, the physician will take a sterile cotton swab and wipe the infected area to try to capture some bacteria.

Remember your experiments where you used a cotton swab to capture bacteria from the surface of your teeth, doorknobs, and hands? The doctor is doing the same thing.

The sample, or culture, will be sent to a clinical laboratory for analysis. Some quick tests have been developed for certain pathogens that can be done at the physician's office, but a sample will always be sent to a laboratory just to make sure. Have you ever had strep throat? There is a rapid test that can be done at the doctor's office to determine whether you are infected with the type of streptococcus that causes strep throat.

At the lab, different tests are applied to the samples. If the lab technicians suspect the pathogen is a bacterium, they will **streak** the sample on different types of bacterial media plates, similar to the ones you've been using for your experiments. How do they streak a sample in a sterile manner?

Have you ever had a throat culture? It's not a very fun experience, but it's an important step to figuring out what microbe you are infected with.

WORDS TO KNOW

inoculate: the process of adding a microbe to a new media plate or flask with liquid growth media.

inoculating loop: a metal tool used to smear bacteria on a growth plate.

Bunsen burner: a gas-lit burner that supplies a constant flame.

Lab technicians take the swab containing the sample and **inoculate** a liquid culture with it, mixing it gently. A tool called an **inoculating loop** is placed in the flame of a **Bunsen burner** until it turns red. Why do you think this is done? What does the heat do? Once cooled, the loop is placed in the mixed liquid culture and some liquid is removed and placed on a bacterial media plate.

There are a lot of bacteria in this small drop of liquid, so the technician will use a certain streaking technique to isolate separate colonies. Here is a picture showing how to streak a bacterial growth plate in a manner that should produce single colonies. Why would they want to isolate separate colonies?

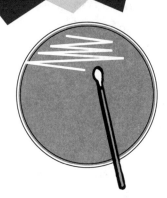   

First set of streaks   Second set of streaks   Third set of streaks   Fourth set of streaks

Technicians can partially identify the bacterium by observing growth on these plates. They also look at the characteristics of the different colonies on the plates. What is the color and size of the colony? Is it wrinkled or smooth? Technicians will also perform chemical tests on the samples before identifying the bacterium.

One of the chemicals used is hydrogen peroxide. You may have seen an adult use hydrogen peroxide on a cut before a bandage was applied. Hydrogen peroxide disinfects cuts, but it is also used in a chemical test to indicate whether a microbe contains the enzyme catalase. Not all bacteria have catalase, so the result gives a clue as to what the suspect bacterium is.

....
Identifying a pathogenic bacteria is like playing a game of 20 questions.
....

Each question answered gives insight into the object, or in this case, the bacterium. The more questions you answer, the better your chances of figuring out what bacterium you are working with. At a certain point, a technician will have enough answered questions to allow them to identify the suspect bacterium with certainty.

Having to grow the bacteria and answer many questions is why the whole process takes several days. If technicians find a different bacterium in the lab than the one the physician thought you were infected with, you'll need to switch to a different medicine.

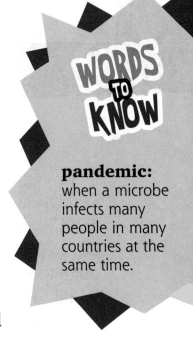

WORDS TO KNOW

pandemic: when a microbe infects many people in many countries at the same time.

• • • OUTBREAKS, EPIDEMICS, AND PANDEMICS • • •

Sometimes, lots of people get sick with the same thing at the same time. If a disease affects more people than expected in a small region, this is called an outbreak. If an infectious disease spreads quickly to many people, it's called an epidemic. A **pandemic** is when a disease spreads across several countries all over the world.

GLOBAL PANDEMIC

During the 1918 Spanish flu pandemic, caused by the influenza virus, between 50 and 100 million deaths occurred. Part of the reason the disease became so widespread was because the world was recovering from World War I and many people were traveling between countries and continents. More people died because of the flu than from fighting in the war.

An organization called the Centers for Disease Control and Prevention (CDC) monitors infections in the United States and helps determine and control outbreaks and epidemics. The World Health Organization (WHO) is the international health agency that determines when a pandemic occurs.

There are several different ways that outbreaks and epidemics can start. Sometimes, a microbe will change by altering something on its surface so that it seems new. This changed microbe can infect a lot more people because no one has been sick with it before. If the microbe had stayed the same and people had been sick with it before, those people would have developed a natural defense against the virus.

Did You Know

The influenza virus usually causes outbreaks, but there have also been several flu pandemics. The worst pandemic occurred in the year 1918, when 500 million people were infected and 50 to 100 million people were killed worldwide.

Our bodies can develop a defense by using their immune systems, or developing immunity, against a pathogen. We will talk about our immune systems and immunity in the next chapter. The influenza virus is an example of a microbe that can change. The influenza virus causes the flu, and it changes every year! That means you have the chance to get sick with the flu each year.

KNOW YOUR MICROBES

INFLUENZA VIRUS (THE FLU)

Viral Pathogen • Infects people and several animals, including pigs and birds

Claim to fame: Nuisance each year, has caused several pandemics

As we learned in Chapter 1, sometimes a microbe is maintained for many years in a reservoir host, such as an animal population. If a person encounters this reservoir population and gets infected, the microbe can spread and infect other people.

After reading all about pathogens, you might be feeling nervous about all the ways there are to get sick! But there are many ways that we can control and prevent the spread of microbes. Let's find out in Chapter 6!

? ESSENTIAL QUESTION

Now it's time to consider and discuss the Essential Question:
How do scientists know that microbes cause illnesses?

DEVELOPING DILUTIONS

IDEAS FOR SUPPLIES
4 or more glasses ✳ *food coloring*

Scientists and medical staff dilute samples of microbes all the time in their experiments or in clinical labs. Often something is diluted by a factor of 10.

1 Label the four glasses *stock, mixture 1, mixture 2,* and *mixture 3.*

2 Pour 1 cup of water in the measuring cup. Add 10 drops of food coloring, any color, to the water. Stir to make sure that the colored water is well mixed.

3 Pour three-quarters of the colored water into the glass labeled *stock.*

4 Add ¾ cup water to the remaining ¼ cup colored water that is left in the measuring cup. Mix well.

5 Pour three-quarters of this colored water into the glass labeled *mixture 1.*

6 Add ¾ cup water to the remaining ¼ cup colored water that is left in the measuring cup. Mix well.

7 Pour three-quarters of this colored water into the glass labeled *mixture 2.*

8 Add ¾ cup water to the remaining ¼ cup colored water that is left in the measuring cup. Mix well.

9 Pour three-quarters of this colored water into the glass labeled *mixture 3.*

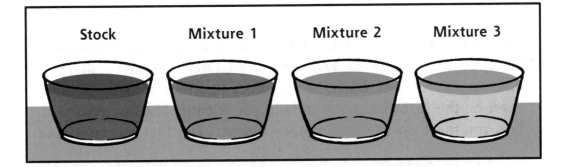

Stock   Mixture 1   Mixture 2   Mixture 3

10 Now analyze the results. Compare all of the glasses to each other. Which liquid is darkest? Which is lightest? Why? Can you fill out the rest of the table to figure out how diluted each mixture is? (Hint: The number is the ratio of colored water to plain water!)

Name on Glass	Dilution Factor
Stock	All stock
Mixture 1	¼ part stock
Mixture 2	
Mixture 3	

Did You Know?

Animals can be a reservoir for viruses. Camels seem to be a reservoir for the MERS virus. Birds have been a reservoir for several strains of the influenza virus.

THINK MORE: If the colored water were a sample of bacteria, what would be happening to the bacteria? Are there more bacteria in the mixture 1 glass or in the mixture 3 glass?

BE A MICROBE DETECTIVE

Dr. Smith needs your help! He has some sick patients arriving for their appointments and he will need to analyze their lab results. Help him determine which bacterium is infecting which patient. Use the chart on the following page to help you identify the bacterium—it gives you the characteristics of each suspect. The first is an example.

1 A little girl has boils on her skin.

Lab results for the little girl:

* gram positive coccus
* positive hydrogen peroxide test

What bacterium should she be treated for? *Staphylococcus aureus*

2 Mr. Icoff Allot has a bad cough.

Lab tests results for Mr. Icoff Allot:

* gram negative coccus
* positive hydrogen peroxide test

What bacterium should he be treated for? _____

3 Mrs. Italle Hurtz has a sore throat, fever, and feels tired.

Lab tests results for Mrs. Italle Hurtz:

* gram positive coccus
* negative hydrogen peroxide test

What bacterium should she be treated for? _____

Bacterium name	Shape of bacterium	Gram stain	Hydrogen peroxide test	Illness caused
Staphylococcus aureus	coccus	positive	positive	Skin infection, upper respiratory infection
Moraxella catarrhalis	diplococcus	negative	positive	Upper & lower respiratory infection
Streptococcus pyogenes	coccus	positive	negative	Upper respiratory infection
Haemophilus influenza	coccus	negative	positive	Upper & lower respiratory infection

FLU SHOT!

Each year, several strains of the influenza virus are included in the flu shot. The CDC estimated that 7.2 million vaccinated people were prevented from getting the flu during the 2013–2014 flu season. This number of people would fit in a straight line from Maine to Oregon! Were you one of these 7.2 million people?

CHAPTER 6

OUR FIGHT AGAINST PATHOGENS

Microbes are the reason we get sick, but we are not defenseless. We have an immune system, vaccines, and many different types of medicines to combat pathogens. Unfortunately, pathogens are also fighting back against our defenses. There is a constant war between our immune system and pathogens.

• • • • • • IMMUNE SYSTEM • • • • • •

Your immune system contains warrior cells that can combat microbes. Many immune cell warriors are available in different parts of your body. When they encounter a microbe, they sound a chemical alarm to recruit other immune cells to the infected area.

We have several types of immune cells that have different functions. Some educate other immune cells. Some can attack and destroy infected cells. Others make sticky molecules that attach to specific microbes, and some gobble up microbes.

? ESSENTIAL QUESTION

How do we fight pathogens?

When the immune system encounters a new microbe, its immune cells study the intruder to figure out how to fight it. This is when you actually feel sick. It might take a while to recover, but if the **incubation period** is long enough, your immune system will be trained to recognize that microbe. You will have an immune memory of this particular microbe. If the immune system comes across this same microbe again, it can clear it quickly from your body without causing you to get sick!

• HOW YOUR IMMUNE SYSTEM WORKS •

When a microbe enters your body, it tries to be as stealthy as it can by hiding inside different cells in your body. Sometimes, a microbe can travel into your body already hiding inside a cell! These sneaky microbes are up to no good.

> Thank goodness your immune cells are patrolling most areas in your body. They will be alerted if something just doesn't seem right.

Depending on how the microbe is found, it can be taken to a command center cell called a **dendritic cell.** This cell will recruit many immune cells by sending out chemical signals. The dendritic cell gives these immune cells information regarding the microbe by displaying a part of the microbe on its surface. Now the recruited immune cells know what to look for. Once they are trained, certain other chemicals cause different immune cells to increase in numbers. These foot soldiers prepare for war against the microbe.

WORDS TO KNOW

incubation period: the period between the infection of an individual by a pathogen and the symptoms of the illness or disease it causes.

dendritic cell: a cell that acts as a command center and alerts immune cells of invading microbes.

97

WORDS TO KNOW

antibodies: unique proteins made by B cells that stick to specific microbes.

regurgitate: to spit up.

Several types of immune cells are trained or recruited to enter a war zone against an intruding pathogen.

Killer T cells: A killer T cell is an immune cell that will hunt down microbes hiding inside body cells. Remember how cells filled with a virus can hang out a flag to let the immune system know they are infected? This is what the killer T cell is looking for. The killer T cell will destroy the cell containing the virus, often before the virus is ready to move on, and the virus will be destroyed with the cell.

B cells: Another type of immune cell, called a B cell, spits out sticky proteins. Called **antibodies**, these sticky proteins bind to specific molecules on the microbe. Often a microbe will be covered in antibodies.

Macrophage cells: A macrophage cell, whose name means "big eater," will gobble up microbes covered with antibodies. The macrophage cell **regurgitates** a portion of the microbe to be displayed on its outside. This is an important part of the immune response against the pathogen. It helps nearby cells prepare for war against the microbe.

These are just a few of the many types of immune cells working together to protect you. Most of the time, your immune system does its job and then reverts to a resting, patrolling state.

It takes a lot of energy for your immune system to engage in an all-out war against a microbe.

Ideally, your body has made an immunological memory. Should this same microbe appear another time, your body will be able to fight it more quickly. Sometimes, your immune system will win the war in such a short time that you will not even be aware that you were infected!

• • • • VACCINES • • • •

Is there a way to avoid these drawn-out battles with pathogenic microbes? There sure is—vaccines!

Dr. Edward Jenner was an English doctor and lifelong bird watcher who lived in the late 1700s. He spent hundreds of hours observing birds and used those same powers of observation when treating his patients. He observed that many of his patients died from smallpox, which is caused by a virus.

Did You Know?

Physicians tried giving people small doses of smallpox to train their immune systems to fight the virus. Unfortunately, this did not work. Most of the people who received the small dose of smallpox got sick and died.

Dr. Jenner noticed that patients who got sick with a cowpox virus never got infected with the smallpox virus. Cowpox is a virus related to smallpox, but people get better from it. Eureka! The cowpox virus could be used as a vaccine against the deadly smallpox virus! Just to be safe, Dr. Jenner spent the next 20 years making observations about cowpox and smallpox infections.

In 1796, Dr. Jenner finally took a chance and vaccinated a young boy with the cowpox virus. To test his theory, he gave the boy the deadly smallpox virus several weeks later. The boy did not get infected with smallpox! This was the first successful vaccine. Since then, the vaccine has saved countless lives. The vaccine works because the smallpox virus and the cowpox virus look similar enough to the immune system to produce an immune memory to protect against both.

Did You Know?

Vaccination comes from the word *vacca*, which means cow. Dr. Jenner used this term to describe inoculating patients with cowpox virus.

KNOW YOUR MICROBES

COWPOX VIRUS

Viral Pathogen • Infects people and cows, but doesn't kill them

Claim to fame: Used to make the first vaccine

SMALLPOX VIRUS (VARIOLA VIRUS)

Viral Pathogen • Infects people and often kills them

Claim to fame: Caused several pandemics and killed many of its victims

You probably do not feel so lucky when you need to get vaccinated. Often the vaccines come in the form of shots. Ouch! Just remember that vaccines prevent you from getting sick, which hurts much worse than a simple shot.

IRRITATING INFLUENZA!

Most vaccines last a lifetime or at least several years. Not so for the influenza vaccine! Do you know why you have to get a yearly flu shot? The influenza virus changes so much each year that our immune system does not recognize it from last year's vaccine.

Each yearly flu shot contains several influenza strains. Scientists and pharmaceutical companies track flu infections each year and use that information to guess which strains will be the most infectious the following year. Have you ever gotten a flu shot only to get sick with the flu anyway? This is because scientists use their best guesses and sometimes don't include all the right strains in the vaccine.

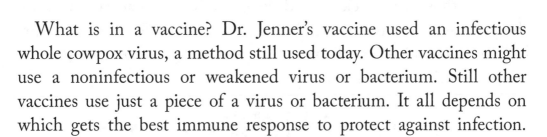

What is in a vaccine? Dr. Jenner's vaccine used an infectious whole cowpox virus, a method still used today. Other vaccines might use a noninfectious or weakened virus or bacterium. Still other vaccines use just a piece of a virus or bacterium. It all depends on which gets the best immune response to protect against infection.

Pharmaceutical companies do a lot of testing to make sure that the vaccine is effective before you ever get it. Each vaccine also has to be approved by the U.S. Food and Drug Administration (FDA). This is a part of the government that screens all drugs and vaccines before they are used on people.

What exactly does a vaccine do for the immune system? It creates an immune memory without your immune system going to war. A vaccine contains a dead microbe or a piece of a microbe that the dendritic cells can use to train different immune cells. The difference is that

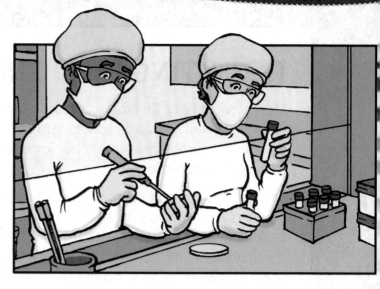

there are no microbes to hunt down or gobble up. Your immune cells are trained and continue to patrol rather than scale up for a full-out war.

A vaccine mimics an infection so your immune cells are trained and ready in case they encounter that infection's microbe.

Some pathogens are so complex that scientists haven't been able to make vaccines to protect against them. In those cases, scientists develop medicines that work against the pathogens differently. Antibiotic medicines work against certain bacteria. **Antiviral** medicines and **antifungal** medicines work against specific viruses and fungi.

• • • • • • • • ANTIBIOTICS • • • • • • •

Scientists in the 1890s observed that certain bacteria and mold did not like to grow together, but their discoveries were largely ignored. Sometimes, getting scientific recognition means being in the right place at the right time.

WORDS TO KNOW

antiviral: medicine that targets a certain virus.

antifungal: medicine that targets certain fungi.

Dr. Alexander Fleming was definitely in the right place at the right time. One day in 1928, he arrived at work to find his bacterial stocks overgrown with a mold. Curiously, the mold and bacteria did not grow on the same place on the plate. In fact, it looked as though the mold was preventing bacteria from growing near it. Dr. Fleming discovered that the mold was inhibiting bacterial growth on several plates. This discovery led to one of the most important medicines of our time—the antibiotic penicillin.

It was a huge task to isolate the antibiotic from the mold. Large amounts were required so that it would be available to anyone who needed it. Penicillin was finally introduced in the 1940s. In 1945, Dr. Fleming shared the Nobel Prize in Medicine with the rest of the scientific team that helped him to prepare penicillin.

Did You Know?

Penicillin only works on certain types of bacteria. In the 1950s, 1960s, and 1970s, more antibiotics were discovered that were effective against different bacteria.

. . . .

Antibiotics save the lives of people with certain infections that would have previously resulted in death.

. . . .

Dr. Fleming warned that overusing antibiotics and antibacterials could lead to bacteria becoming unaffected by them. He was absolutely right. In the late 1930s, certain bacterial strains were already **resistant** to the antibacterial medicine sulfonamide.

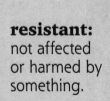

WORDS TO KNOW

resistant: not affected or harmed by something.

WORDS TO KNOW

resistance gene: a piece of DNA that gives the microbe the ability to be resistant.

When a bacterium becomes resistant to an antibiotic, that antibiotic no longer works on that particular bacterium. A bacterium can become resistant to an antibiotic when it acquires a **resistance gene**. This is a small piece of genetic material that codes for a certain protein.

A bacterium will make a protein from the genetic material that will in some manner block the action of a particular antibiotic. If a bacterium can block an antibiotic, it will be unaffected by the antibiotic and is said to be resistant to the antibiotic. Bacteria can share resistance genes with other bacteria. This happens randomly between bacteria, but is more likely to happen if a patient does not follow instructions to finish their antibiotic medication.

"BUT I 'FEEL' FINE . . . "

When you take an antibiotic to treat an illness, you might be tempted to stop taking your prescription when you feel better. However, even when you feel better, there are still some bacteria being chased down by the medicine. Not finishing your medication may result in a bacterium becoming resistant to the antibiotic in your body.

This new bacterium may be sensitive to a different antibiotic, so you can take a different medicine. Unfortunately for some patients, there may not be any more choices of antibiotics available, which means they will remain infected. This is happening more often as more bacteria develop resistance to antibiotics. It is important to finish taking the antibiotic medicine that your doctor prescribes, unless you have a bad reaction to the medicine. If that happens, you need to go back to your physician for a different medication.

How does a scientist know if a bacterium is sensitive or resistant to an antibiotic?

They use a method similar to Dr. Fleming's. Researchers streak bacteria onto the entire space of several growth plates. Then they place an antibiotic pill in the center of the plate. The bacteria are allowed to grow for several days.

zone of inhibition: the area around an antibiotic that is free of bacterial growth.

The area around the antibiotic where no bacteria grow is called the **zone of inhibition**. Researchers measure and compare the zones of inhibition of several antibiotics against the same bacterium. The antibiotic with the largest zone of inhibition is the best antibiotic to give to patients. Why do you think that is?

• • • • ANTIVIRALS AND ANTIFUNGALS • • • •

Just as there are medicines against bacteria, there are also medicines against certain viruses and fungi. Antiviral and antifungal medications work differently from antibiotics. Each medicine works in its own unique way to either block a specific microbe from making more of itself or by directly injuring the microbe.

Did You Know?

Have you ever had athlete's foot? You might have used an antifungal cream to get rid of it.

Antivirals only work against viruses, and each antiviral is effective against only a specific virus. Some patients need to take antiviral medications for years. Antifungal medications only work against certain fungi. Most antifungal medications are creams for your skin and are not to be swallowed.

HUMAN IMMUNODEFICIENCY VIRUS (HIV)

Viral Pathogen • Infects people and causes aquired immune deficiency syndrome (AIDS)

Claim to fame: HIV killed humans before a drug was found that could block HIV production while keeping the patient alive.

Did You Know?

People infected with human immunodeficiency virus (HIV) need to take several antiviral medications for many years.

We are very lucky to live in a time when we have access to many different vaccines and medicines that keep us healthy. What else can you do to keep the pathogens away? The best thing to do besides getting your vaccines is to wash your hands!

The amount of time that you wash your hands matters too. Make sure to wash them for at least 20 seconds with plenty of warm water and soap.

? ESSENTIAL QUESTION

Now it's time to consider and discuss the Essential Question: How do we fight pathogens?

FLU MADLIB

Use the parts of speech and as many glossary words as you can to fill in the blanks and complete this silly story!

Last year, I got so sick from the flu that I had to lie in bed for _____ weeks. (NUMBER)
My _____ ached, I had a runny _____ and a cough that sounded (BODY PART) (BODY PART)
like _____. My mother also said that my face looked _____. (NOISE) (COLOR)

This year is going to be different. I don't want to be sick. I made an
appointment with Dr. _____ to get a flu shot. I am scared, but would rather (NOUN)
get something that feels like a pinch than lie in _____ sick again. My (FURNITURE AT HOME)
friend _____ said, "_____, I can't believe that you are getting a (FRIEND'S NAME) (EXCLAMATION)
shot. I'm not going to."

My mom took me to the doctor's office. I was feeling _____, but I tried to (ADJECTIVE)
be brave. I didn't look while the nurse gave me the shot. My doctor came in
and shook my _____. "Good job! You were brave," she said. "You can pick (BODY PART)
out a _____ from our basket up front." I went home feeling proud of myself. (NOUN)

One day in school, three weeks later, my friend started to feel sick
during _____ class. "Wow, your face looks _____," I said. My friend (SCHOOL SUBJECT) (COLOR)
looked upset and said, "I don't feel well. My _____ is runny and (BODY PART)
my _____ hurts. I hope I don't have the flu!" "_____, I wish you had (BODY PART) (EXCLAMATION)
gotten a flu shot with me!" I said as my friend went to the nurse.

WASH YOUR HANDS!

IDEAS FOR SUPPLIES

4 prepared media plates ✳ *soap* ✳ *antibacterial liquid* ✳ *plastic wrap* ✳ *heat wrap*

1 Take four prepared media plates out of the refrigerator. Let them sit for an hour at room temperature.

2 Do not wash your hands! Play with your pets, run around outside, and touch many things before you do this experiment! The dirtier your hands the better!

3 Choose a media plate. Gently place your hand on the surface. Do not push into the media too hard or some gelatin will break off. Cover the container with plastic wrap, label it *dirty hand*. Put this in the incubator upside down. If you have a heat wrap, use it now.

4 Have someone wash your right hand with soap and water for 20 seconds. Choose a new media plate and gently place your right hand on the surface. Cover the container, label it *soap*, and place it upside down in the incubator.

5 Repeat step 4 with your left hand and antibacterial liquid. Make sure they wash your hand for 20 seconds. Label the container *antibacterial*, and place it upside down in the incubator.

6 To prepare the negative control, label a media plate *negative control*. Remove the lid, wrap the top, and place it in the incubator upside down.

7 Record your experiment and materials used in your science journal. What is your hypothesis? What kind of microbes do you think will grow and on which plates will they grow?

8 Look at your plates, but don't unwrap them. Record your results at 24, 48, and 72 hours. Record your observations about how many colonies grew and what you notice about each one.

THINK MORE: Are your results as expected? Is this experiment going to change the way you wash your hands in the future? Do you think washing your hands for longer or shorter periods of time will give you different results?

SULFONAMIDE

Although penicillin was the first antibiotic discovered, it was not the first medicine available to patients. The very first antibacterial made available to patients, called sulfonamide, arrived in 1937. It was discovered in 1932 by Gerhard Domagk, a German bacteriologist and pathologist. He observed that a red dye, called Prontosil, cured a certain bacterial infection in mice. Mice given the red dye changed the dye into an active drug in their bodies. The active drug cured the mice of their bacterial infection. In 1939, Dr. Domagk received the Nobel Prize in Medicine for his discovery of the antibacterial sulfonamide.

HERD IMMUNITY

Herd immunity occurs when an entire population is protected against a particular microbe even though some people have not been vaccinated. How does this work? Here is a simple game to demonstrate the process. Orange squares represent people who got the flu shot, white squares are those who did not. The flu virus enters the herd through the outside edges.

SITUATION #1 ➔

* ✱ 4 people did not get the flu shot
* ✱ 45 people got the flu shot

How many might get infected by the flu virus?

Zero!

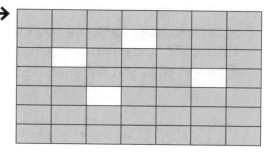

SITUATION #2 ➔

* ✱ 8 people did not get the flu shot
* ✱ 41 people did get the flu shot

How many might get infected by the flu virus?

_____

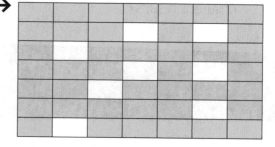

SITUATION #3 ➔

* ✱ 16 did not get the flu shot
* ✱ 33 did get the flu shot

How many might get infected by the flu virus?

_____

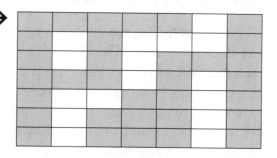

SITUATION #4 ⟶

* 32 did not get the flu shot
* 17 did get the flu shot

How many might get infected by the flu virus?

_____

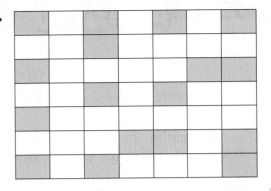

THINK MORE: Why do you think herd immunity works? Can you draw a new Situation #3 so that no one will become infected with the influenza virus? Why or why not? Can you draw a new Situation #4 so that no one will become infected with the influenza virus? Why or why not?

WORDS TO KNOW

bacteriophage: a virus that infects bacteria.

ADVANCES IN ANTIBIOTICS

Scientists are trying to come up with new antibiotics to use against bacteria. It is not easy. For the last 50 years, research has yielded very little. Recently, two groups have come up with unique ways to find or make new antibiotics. One group has made a modified **bacteriophage** that targets or kills only antibiotic-resistant bacteria. A bacteriophage is a virus that infects only bacteria. What a terrific idea—using a pathogenic microbe to kill another pathogenic microbe!

Another group has figured out a way to use microbes that cannot be cultured in the laboratory. By growing microbes in their natural habitat, the soil, scientists have found a promising new antibiotic!

AMAZING ANTIBIOTICS

IDEAS FOR SUPPLIES
3 prepared media plates ✴ *lemon with green mold from Chapter 4 experiment*

Remember how Dr. Alexander Fleming discovered penicillin? You might get similar results with your own experiment!

1 Take three prepared media plates out of the refrigerator. Let them warm up for an hour at room temperature.

2 Wash your hands! Your experiments won't be sterile, but keeping your hands clean will allow you to get good results.

3 To prepare the negative control, label a media plate *negative control*, remove the lid, and wrap the top with plastic wrap, using a rubber band to keep the plastic wrap in place. Place the negative control in the incubator upside down.

4 Take a cotton swab and wet it slightly with water. Swab different places around the house, such as doorknobs, the sink, and under faucets.

5 Choose two new media plates. Gently place the swab on the surface of the media and swipe it back and forth over the entire surfaces on both plates. Do not push the swab into the media too hard or some gelatin will break off. Throw the swab away. Cover one container with plastic wrap and a rubber band and label *fomites*. Put this in the incubator upside down.

6 Retrieve the moldy lemon from the experiment in Chapter 2. Open the bag just enough to reach a new swab to touch a part of the mold on the lemon. Do not put your face near the bag or breathe in the mold. Touch this swab to the center of the second media plate just one time. No swabbing back and forth! Throw away the moldy swab. Quickly cover the media container with plastic wrap and a rubber band and label it *fomites + mold*. Put this in the incubator upside down.

7 Record your experiment in your science journal. What is your hypothesis? What kind of microbes do you think will grow? Which area will produce more microbes? What do you think the mold will do?

8 Look at your plates, but do not unwrap them. Record your results at 24 hours, 48 hours, and 72 hours. Write down how many different types of microbes you see and what they look like. Add details about the mold.

THINK MORE: How did the mold affect the bacteria? Why did it behave this way? What does that tell you about how antibiotics work in your own body against pathogens?

HELP NEEDED IN THE LABORATORY!

A laboratory needs your help! A new technician has started to work here and does not know how to read the results of an antibiotic sensitivity test. Take a look at the test results and decide which antibiotic each patient should get.

Antibiotic Testing:

* Black Antibiotic
* Red Antibiotic
* Green Antibiotic

Negative Control

(no bacterial growth)

Positive Control

(bacteria growth covering entire plate)

PATIENT #1:

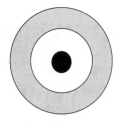 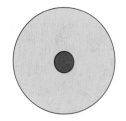 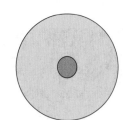

PATIENT #2:

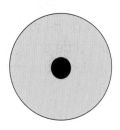 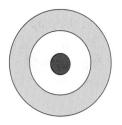 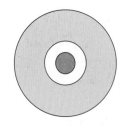

THINK MORE: Why do you think a whole plate of bacteria has to be grown? Do you think that more than three antibiotics should be tested against the sample from each patient? Why or why not?

acidic: from acids, which are chemical compounds that taste sour, bitter, or tart. Examples are vinegar and lemon juice.

aerobic: an environment with oxygen.

anaerobic: an environment with low oxygen or no oxygen.

antibiotic: a medicine that can disable or kill bacteria.

antibodies: unique proteins made by B cells that stick to specific microbes.

antifungal: medicine that targets certain fungi.

antiseptic: using clean and sterile methods to do any microbiological procedure.

antiviral: medicine that targets a certain virus.

archaea: a single-celled microbe that lives in extremely harsh environments.

atmosphere: the blanket of air surrounding the earth.

bacteria: a microbe found in animals, plants, soil, and water that can be a symbiont or pathogen.

bacteriology: the study of bacteria.

bacteriophage: a virus that infects bacteria.

biofilm: a sheet of bacteria.

biofuel: fuel made from living matter, such as plants.

bioremediation: the process of using biological organisms to clean up a polluted area.

Bunsen burner: a gas-lit burner that supplies a constant flame.

carbolic acid: a powerful antimicrobial and disinfectant.

carbon dioxide: an odorless, colorless gas formed from the burning of fossil fuels, the rotting of dead plants and animals, and when animals breathe out.

carnivorous: a plant or animal that eats meat. Some plants trap and digest small animals, mostly insects.

categorize: to put things into different groups based on their characteristics.

cell: the most basic part of a living thing. Billions of cells make up a plant or animal.

cell membrane: the membrane surrounding the cytoplasm of a cell.

cell wall: the layer outside the membrane of a cell.

cilia: hair-like extensions that help a microbe move in a certain direction or attach to a surface.

classify: to put things in groups based on what they have in common.

colonize: to move into and live in.

compensate: to do something positive to counter a negative effect.

conidia: colorful spores released by fungi that enable the fungi to grow in a different area.

consumption: using something.

contagion: an unseen particle that is infectious.

culture: to grow a microbe in growth media.

curd: a solid chunk of milk protein.

curdle: when milk protein clumps together due to acidity.

cytoplasm: the thick fluid inside a cell.

decomposer: any organism that breaks down dead or decaying organic matter.

dehydrate: to take the water out of something.

dendritic cell: a cell that acts as a command center and alerts immune cells of invading microbes.

115

disintegrate: the process of falling apart and being destroyed.

DNA: the acronym for deoxyribonucleic nucleic acid. DNA is genetic material that contains instructions that makes us who we are.

drought: a long period of time when it doesn't rain as much as usual.

ecosystem: a community of living and nonliving things. Living things are plants, animals, and insects. Nonliving things are soil, rocks, and water.

endospore: a small, inactive version of a bacterium that can survive harsh conditions.

environment: the area in which something lives.

enzyme: a protein that speeds up a chemical reaction.

epidemic: the rapid spread of a microbe that causes a large population of people to become sick in a short period of time.

eradicate: to get rid of forever.

evaporation: the process of a liquid heating up and changing into a gas, such as water vapor.

extract: to remove something.

ferment: when microorganisms convert sugars into acids.

filamented: a series of cells that form a long, chain-like structure.

filtration: passing liquid through a filter to clean it of particles.

flagellum: a very long hair that moves in a whip-like motion to move a bacterium forward.

flora: the symbiotic microbes that reside in different parts of the body.

fomite: a nonliving object that can carry microbes.

food web: a complex set of feeding relationships between plants and animals.

fossil fuels: oil, natural gas, and coal, which are natural fuels that formed long ago from the remains of living organisms.

freshwater: an aquatic system, such as a lake, pond, stream, or river, with water that is not salty.

fungi: a plant-like microbe without leaves or flowers that grows on other plants or decaying material. Examples are mold, mildew, and mushrooms.

genetic: relating to genes, which are units of DNA and RNA that assign organisms their characteristics.

global warming: an increase in the average temperature of the earth's atmosphere, enough to cause climate change.

greenhouse gas: a gas such as water vapor, carbon dioxide, or methane that traps heat and contributes to warming temperatures.

habitat: a plant or animal's home, which supplies it with food, water, and shelter.

halophile: a salt-loving organism.

host: an organism that can be infected by a microbe.

humidity: the amount of moisture in the air.

hyphae: long shapes on some fungi that serve as the main place of growth.

immobile: not capable of moving.

immune system: a system in your body that removes pathogens.

inclusion: parts of a microbe.

incubation period: the period between the infection of an individual by a pathogen and the symptoms of the illness or disease it causes.

infect: to invade, to cause someone or something to become sick.

116

infectious: capable of causing an infection.

inoculate: the process of adding a microbe to a new media plate or flask with liquid growth media.

inoculating loop: a metal tool used to smear bacteria on a growth plate.

legume: a plant with seeds that grow in pods, such as peas and beans.

luminescent: glowing.

marine: found in the ocean.

media plate: a dish that contains a growth medium for growing microbes in a laboratory.

methanogen: an organism that produces methane gas.

microbe: a tiny living or nonliving thing.

microbial mat: several layers of biofilm.

microorganism: a living thing that is so small you can only see it with a microscope.

mycelium: a large web of hyphae.

mycology: the study of fungi.

nitrogen fixation: the process of turning nitrogen gas into a liquid.

nodule: a small rounded swelling.

nutrients: substances in food and soil that living things need to live and grow.

opaque: not transparent.

organic: something that is or was living.

organism: any living thing.

outbreak: an expected seasonal rise in the number of infections in one area.

pandemic: when a microbe infects many people in many countries at the same time.

parasitic: living on another plant or animal and feeding off of it.

pathogen: a microbe that exists only to take advantage of other organisms. Pathogens can cause disease or even death in that organism.

photic zone: the top layer of water, which receives the most sunlight.

photosynthesis: the process of using light and carbon dioxide to make food and energy for the organism.

predator: an animal that hunts another animal for food.

polyhedron: a shape with many sides.

protist: a group of microbes that include the protozoans, most algae, and often slime molds.

protistology: the study of protists.

receptor: a protein on a cell that serves as a lock by interacting with a viral key.

regurgitate: to spit up.

reproduce: to make something new, just like itself.

reservoir: a host, such as an animal, plant, insect, or person, that maintains, but does not get sick from, a microbe.

resistance gene: a piece of DNA that gives the microbe the ability to be resistant.

resistant: not affected or harmed by something.

rhizobia: special bacteria that live in nodules growing off a legume's plant root.

ribosome: parts of a cell that construct proteins.

RNA: the acronym for ribonucleic acid. RNA is genetic material that contains the code to make a certain protein.

secretions: fluid produced by our bodies.

sewage: waste from buildings, carried away through sewers. A sewer is a drain for waste.

species: a group of plants or animals that are closely related and look the same.

spoilage: rotting or rotted.

spore: a single cell that can produce an organism.

sterile: free from microorganisms.

sterilize: to make clean and free of any microbes.

streak: a process of smearing bacteria on a growth plate.

susceptible: easily influenced or affected by something.

symbiont: a microorganism that exists in harmony with another organism. Both gain benefits from this relationship.

theory: an unproven scientific idea.

thermophile: a heat-loving organism.

vaccine: a preparation containing part of or a whole microbe given to a patient to prevent disease.

vector: something that can carry a microbe from one organism to another.

virology: the study of viruses.

virus: a small infectious microbe that can replicate only inside the living cells of an organism.

waste: garbage.

zone of inhibition: the area around an antibiotic that is free of bacterial growth.

METRIC EQUIVALENTS

Use this chart to find the metric equivalents to the English measurements in this book. If you need to know a half measurement, divide by two. If you need to know twice the measurement, multiply by two. How do you find a quarter measurement? How do you find three times the measurement?

English	Metric
1 inch	2.5 centimeters
1 foot	30.5 centimeters
1 yard	0.9 meter
1 mile	1.6 kilometers
1 pound	0.5 kilogram
1 teaspoon	5 milliliters
1 tablespoon	15 milliliters
1 cup	237 milliliters

BOOKS AND ARTICLES

Brock, Thomas D. *Milestones in Microbiology.* Prentice Hall International Inc. 1961.

Cano, R.J., et al. *Revival and Identification of Bacterial Spores in 25- to 40-Million-Year-Old Dominican Amber.* Science. 268:1060-64, 1995.

Citorik, R., et al. *Sequence-specific antimicrobials using efficiently delivered RNA-guided nucleases.* Nature Biotechnology. 32:1141-45, 2014.

Eckburg et al. *Archaea and Their Potential Role in Human Disease.* Infection and Immunity. 591-596, 2003.

Hingorani, K.S., and Gierasch, L.M. *How Bacteria Survive an Acid Trip.* Proceedings of National Academy of Sciences. 110:5279-80, 2013.

Hotz, R.L. *Big Data and Bacteria: Mapping the New York Subway's DNA.* The Wall Street Journal. Feb 5, 2015.

Jenner, Edward. *The Three Original Publications on Vaccination Against Smallpox.* The Harvard Classics. 1909-14.

Katz, Laura A. *Origin and Diversification of Eukaryotes.* Annual Review of Microbiology. 66:411-27, 2009.

Koopman, M.M., et al. *The Carnivorous Pale Pitcher Plant Harbors Diverse, Distinct and Time-Dependent Bacterial Communities.* Applied and Environmental Microbiology. 76:1851-60, 2010.

Ling, L.L., et al. *A New Antibiotic Kills Pathogens Without Detectable Resistance.* Nature. 2015.

Madigan, M., et al. *Brock Biology of Microorganisms.* Benjamin Cummings. 13th edition, 2010.

National Institutes of Health/National Institutes of Allergy and Infectious Diseases: niaid.nih.gov/news/newsreleases/2014/pages/camelsmers-cov.aspx

Paul, E.A., and Clark, F.E. *Soil Microbiology and Biochemistry.* Academic Press. 1996.

Reynolds, Moira D. *How Pasteur Changed History.* McGuinn & McGuire Publishing Inc. 1994.

Rogan, Brian, et al. *Exploring the Sulfur Nutrient Cycle: Using the Winogradsky Column.* The American Biology Teacher. 67,6: 348-356, 2005.

Santer, Melvin. *Joseph Lister: First Use of a Bacterium as a 'Model Organism' to Illustrate the Cause of Infectious Disease in Humans.* Notes and Records of the Royal Society Journal of History of Science. 64:59-65, 2010.

Stephenson, Steven L. *The Kingdom Fungi: The Biology of Mushrooms, Molds, and Lichens.* Timber Press, 2010.

Van Elsas, J.D., Jansson, J.K., Trevors, J.T. *Modern Soil Microbiology.* CRC Press, 2006.

Vreeland, R.H., et al. *Isolation of a 250 Million Year Old Halotolerant Bacterium From a Primary Salt Crystal.* Nature. 407:897-900, 2000.

Zimmer, C. *How Microbes Defend and Define Us.* The New York Times. July 12, 2010.

WEBSITES

American Society for Microbiology: asm.org

Centers for Disease Control and Prevention: cdc.gov

Biology 4 Kids: biology4kids.com/files/micro_main.html

Microbe World: archives.microbeworld.org/resources/experiment.aspx

Howard Hughes Medical Institute: media.hhmi.org/biointeractive/films/Seeing-the-Invisible.html

More resources for *Microbes* available at www.nomadpress.net

QR CODE INDEX

ESSENTIAL QUESTIONS

Chapter 1: What kinds of environments do different types of microbes live in?

Chapter 2: What are microbes doing in and on your body?

Chapter 3: Why are microbes an important part of aquatic ecosystems?

Chapter 4: What purpose do microbes serve in soil and in the air?

Chapter 5: How do scientists know that microbes cause illnesses?

Chapter 6: How do we fight a pathogen?